Compassionate Presence

Compassionate Presence

A Radical Response to Human Suffering

Rolf R. Nolasco Jr.
with R. Vincent MacDonald

Foreword by
Andrew Dreitcer

CASCADE *Books* · Eugene, Oregon

COMPASSIONATE PRESENCE
A Radical Response to Human Suffering

Cascade Books
An Imprint of Wipf and Stock Publishers
199 W. 8th Ave., Suite 3
Eugene, OR 97401

www.wipfandstock.com

PAPERBACK ISBN: 978-1-4982-0203-9
HARDCOVER ISBN: 978-1-4982-8754-8
EBOOK ISBN: 978-1-4982-0204-6

Cataloguing-in-Publication data:

Names: Nolasco, Rolf R., Jr., with R. Vincent MacDonald.

Title: Compassionate presence : a radical response to human suffering / Rolf R. Nolasco Jr. with R. Vincent MacDonald.

Description: Eugene, OR: Cascade Books, 2016 | Series: if applicable | Includes bibliographical references and index.

Identifiers: ISBN 978-1-4982-0203-9 (paperback) | ISBN 978-1-4982-8754-8 (hardcover) | ISBN 978-1-4982-0204-6 (ebook)

Subjects: LCSH: 1. Compassion. 2. Suffering. 3. Psychotherapy. I. Title.

Classification: BJ1475 .N627 2016 (print) | BJ1475 (ebook)

Manufactured in the U.S.A. OCTOBER 18, 2016

Interior image: Vincent van Gogh's "The Good Samaritan" (Wikimedia Commons PD-Art).

Table of Contents

Foreword

ALMOST FIFTEEN YEARS AGO my late wife, Wendy, was diagnosed with brain cancer. She was a Presbyterian minister, a noted preacher, a beloved pastor—and the mother of two girls in their early teens. Soon after the tumor appeared she lost much of her short-term memory, half her vision, and her ability to manage her daily life. Eventually she was unable to walk without the benefit of a cane or a loved one's arm. Most days found her in bed or simply resting.

But she kept preaching. Yes, all through the ten months of her cancer she kept preaching, right up until some days before her death. She preached through Ordinary Time, Advent, Christmas, and Lent, and was supposed to preach on Easter Sunday—but couldn't get out of bed that morning. She slept, instead. And soon entered her own resurrection.

Each week during her illness Wendy prepared for her sermon with my help. Her process looked like this: she asked me what the lectionary texts were, let an idea come to her in that moment, and instructed me on what research to do to provide background on the topic. So I did her research. I read my findings aloud to her. She guided me in further research, if necessary. And then, unable to write or type, she constructed a sermon in her mind.

Every Saturday evening Wendy would ask me (as she did at the end of every day), "What day is it?" "Saturday," I'd say. "Am I preaching tomorrow?" she'd ask. "Yes" I'd say. But by that point she had no memory of her sermon topic. No memory of it at all. She would be anxious for a while. But then even the thought of preaching would pass—until I reminded her the next morning that she was scheduled to be in the pulpit. We would go to church, and still she had no recollection of what she had meant to say. That would be the case right up until she sat down in front of the congregation to deliver her message.

Then she would remember. And she would preach for an hour. Lucid-ly. Brilliantly. Beautifully. Profoundly. With no sign of short-term memory loss, and with her vision seemingly restored, she occasionally called out to people she noticed in the congregation, drawing everyone into her words of grace. Wendy's sermons packed the sanctuary Sunday after Sunday.

The church members and visitors said of her preaching, "It's the Holy Spirit." The neuro-oncologist said, "There's a tumor in the occipital lobe."

What was going on here? Was Wendy's Sunday morning brilliance her brain on God? Or on cancer? Or neither? Or both?

And then, of course, there was the compassion. It came in floods. Family members began arriving to lend a hand. The wider community joined efforts to deliver food, ferry our daughters from place to place, and provide a constant presence in the house when I could not be there. Wishes for healing, prayers for wholeness, and gifts of grace came from congregations and convents, friends of friends, and folks completely unknown to us from across the country and around the globe.

And the compassion came not only *to* Wendy, but *from* Wendy. Church members and others came to her bedside to receive pastoral care. Or they phoned her for words of compassionate wisdom. During those visits or calls Wendy was fully present, the warm, caring, no-nonsense spiritual counselor she had always been. And then, more often than not, she would sleep—until the next pastoral call.

What was going on here? Where did all of this compassion come from? How was Wendy able to conjure it up from the midst of her exhaustion? How did mass quantities of compassion suddenly appear from the world around us and beyond? What prompted and sustained it? Was it God? Or bodies responding naturally? Or the pressure of cultural and religious re-sponsibilities? Or none of these? Or all of them?

I relate this story of pain and miracles and questions because for me it crystallizes the vital concerns of the book you are about to read. In these pages Nolasco and MacDonald tackle head on complex issues that were raised (vividly) by my wife's cancer and (more subtly) by my daily efforts (and yours, perhaps) to live a life that is faithful to Divine Love. Chris-tians and others have struggled with such issues across time, continents, and cultures: What is the nature of compassion? Why am I compassionate to some people and not to others? Why in some times and not in others? Which part of my life comes from my own efforts and which part is Divine Compassion working in me? What is the relationship between my brain and my mind, and between these two and God's work in my life? Where does my body fit into this? In health? In sickness? How can compassion sustain me in times of stress, trauma, and pain? What keeps me from a path of compassion? What helps me become more compassionate?

To address such questions, Nolasco and MacDonald skillfully draw on the ancient wisdom of Scripture, theologians, and spiritual sages. But I am pleased to say that they also offer us wisdom from new sources. That is, they plumb the insights of the most up-to-date understandings of cognitive neuroscientists, neuropsychologists, social neuroscientists, and neurophysiologists. Just as the ancients addressed burning faith questions with the best science of their eras, Nolasco and MacDonald apply to such questions the best scientific understandings of our own era. What's more, they do this not in conflict with faith, but to help us know how to respond more completely to the Divine invitation to compassion. Through this enlightening mix of the old and the new, we come to see (among other things) how brain research relates to taking on the mind of Christ; how current understandings of emotion illuminate the compassion of Jesus, how moral rules can be appropriately understood in light of how our brains and bodies work; and how compassion grows through mindful attention to our feelings, our physical states, and our stances toward others.

As I look back over the period of my late wife's illness, I recognize that I would have been greatly helped at that time by what Nolasco and MacDonald offer us in these pages. It isn't that they would have definitively answered all my questions; no one can know for sure what the ravages of cancer bring or how the Spirit of compassion moves in, through, and around that trauma. Some things remain mysteries in our lives. But they do give me a new way to see such things, new perspectives on how compassion flows from, interacts with, and transforms even the most difficult of situations. Had I known then what Nolasco and MacDonald have now taught me, I could have been more present, grounded, and stable in my care-giving. They show me how I might find appropriate, courageous, compassionate ways forward in the face of the worst that life might bring. For in the pages of their book I find ways to settle into Divine Compassion—vital for sustaining strength and hope when the world around us seems to be crumbling. And I find ways to cultivate compassion for myself—necessary for those of us who never live up to our own expectations. And I discover ways to form compassion for others—required if we are to "love our enemies."

In short, I feel blessed to have such an illuminating, wise, practical guide to radical compassion in response to human suffering. And I trust that you will feel the same.

Andrew Dreitcer
Claremont School of Theology

Acknowledgements

As the traditional African saying goes, "it takes a village to raise a child." This little book maybe the brainchild of a singular person but it has taken a whole village to turn it into something useful and hopefully edifying and transforming. In this village we were accompanied by several individuals whose encouragement and direction kept us focused, inspired, and committed to finish this task with delight and enthusiasm—David Johnson, Stan Hamm, Lissa Wray-Beal, Rod Lantin, and the staff at Tyndale House and Faraday Institute for Science and Religion in Cambridge, England.

We were also taught greatly by our students at Providence Theological Seminary, our clients and fellow parishioners whose perseverance and resilience during their darkest hour has served as a source of light and revelation during the writing process. To the editorial staff at Wipf & Stock, especially Matthew Wimer and Rodney Clapp, thank you for believing in this project.

Lastly, our journey would not have reached its destination without the quiet and reassuring presence of our families whose love and belief in us buoyed us forward into the completion of this book.

Soli Deo Gloria.

Introduction

"Hello, I am Baymax, your personal healthcare companion,"[1] says the white inflatable robot to Hiro Hamada upon hearing his cry of distress. Created by Hiro's older brother Tadashi, Baymax assesses his patient's condition, tends to his wounds, and offers him a lollipop for being a good boy. The plump and huggable robot then gives Hiro the code words to deactivate him—"I am satisfied with my care"—which he utters in confusion and disbelief.

There lies the beginning of a beautiful friendship between the two principal characters of the movie *Big Hero 6*. This exchange also captures Baymax's raison d'être, that is, to heal the sick and injured, those within his presence. In more clinical terms, as a healthcare robot, his sole purpose is to respond to suffering through timely and accurate assessment and informed and effective intervention until health or well-being of the patient is regained or restored. The healing practice is carried out in a non-threatening manner as evidenced by his calm reassuring voice and soft and cushy appearance—Baymax is "a big marshmallow" as Hiro describes him. His companionship provides comfort and assurance and his intent to help knows no bounds.

Tadashi's genius creation of a healthcare robot is meant to address the ubiquitous nature of suffering as experienced by the residents of the archetypal city San Fransyoko. Universal themes of loss, greed, deceit, self-ishness, and revenge are intertwined with the human thirst and satisfying nature of faithful companionship afforded by Hiro's best friends and Tadashi's former colleagues at the nerd school, namely, Honey Lemon, Go Go Tomago, Wasabi, and Fred. Together with Hiro and Baymax they constitute the titular Big Hero 6, whose meteoric rise to fame as protectors and saviors of the city is endearingly predictable yet funny and captivating. It will leave the viewer wanting for his own personal healthcare companion, perhaps a

1. *Big Hero 6.*

1

human version of Baymax's core trait of compassionate presence, especially during times of distress and suffering.

Through yet another film this outpouring of compassion during times of great need is embodied by Pastor Jay Reinke, which is chronicled in the feature-length documentary film entitled *The Overnighters*.[2] As the minister of Concordia Lutheran Church Pastor Jays takes on the formidable task of opening the church's doors to a throng of unemployed strangers in search for a better life in the oil boom town of Williston, North Dakota. As it turns out their American dream quickly became a nightmare when the grim reality of scant job prospects and absence of housing descended upon them.

Sensing an urgency to meet a pressing need and driven by passion, faith, and commitment to the call of Christ, Pastor Jay and members of this local church transposed its building into a makeshift dwelling. "There is room in the inn" for those displaced by the lure of economic prosperity. Day in and day out the "overnighters," as Pastor Jay calls them, now have a place to lay their heads as they work or continue to look for work. The central tenet of Christian hospitality to the strangers is vivified through the outstretched arms of embrace extended to those who need it the most.

Everybody happy? Not quite, as that is only half of the story. As the ministry to the overnighters continues and evolves, the cracks that are hidden underneath the walls of the church and the community at large are laid bare. The secret and checkered lives of some of the overnighters are soon revealed. Indeed, a perfect storm is brewing and it is about to make landfall on this unsuspecting midwestern community.

Some members of Concordia Lutheran started to raise their concerns over the optics and outcomes of hosting itinerant laborers and unemployed into their fold. The city council, armed with political voice and power, imposed its will upon Pastor Jay and ordered him to shut the program down. Pressures from all sides weighed heavily on this self-sacrificing shepherd of the flock and wandering sheep. Not long after, the pastor's own wounds and struggles tucked away for so long and conveniently by ministry duties and priorities began to surface and pester. All these conspired against the noblest intention to show compassion by well-meaning individuals, who find themselves at odds with each other's beliefs and priorities. In the midst of this personal, societal, and spiritual quagmire, the overnighters are left to fend for themselves and Pastor Jay is forced to confront his own pain.

2. *The Overnighters.*

INTRODUCTION

Wouldn't it be nice to have the Big Hero 6 make an appearance in Williston, North Dakota! At least, within the realm of playful imagination, Baymax and his cohort can wipe out the pain and suffering that the central characters are grappling with in that riveting and layered documentary film. But that would be wishful thinking, wouldn't it? However, what is not beyond imagination and blatantly clear in real life is the fact that human suffering is all around us and that we have the innate capacity to alleviate and transform it through acts of compassion. Both films address this twin reality within the confines of the medium in which they are presented. Hence, they are limited in breadth and scope yet good enough to crack wide open these themes that demand further exploration and nuanced description.

This little book is an attempt at doing exactly that—to provide a thick description of compassion from the rich tradition of theology, psychology, and brain science. Compassion is something that people experience especially when confronted with the stark reality of suffering. This subjective experience is layered and littered with specific emotional states, thought processes, and behavioral responses that can be disentangled and understood more fully. Though acts of compassion can easily be spotted, its underpinnings are far more complex yet encouragingly discernible.

Like any human experience, compassion has a neurological basis. With advances in neuroscience, brain networks responsible for the experience of compassion have now been identified and mapped. Certainly, this has a huge bearing not only in understanding the neural correlates of compassion but also in designing specific practices that help strengthen these neural wirings. Based on the intertwining components of compassion alone it behooves us to approach this subject matter from an integrative perspective. As said previously, we are drawing from the rich reservoir of complementary disciplines that have offered significant insights into this issue, albeit in separate quarters and independent of each other. By bridging these disciplines into one coherent and coordinated whole we offer more extensive and penetrating coverage on the subject matter than is possible through single disciplinary means. This effort is inspired by those who blazed the trail in relating religion and theology with brain science, with astounding and pragmatic outcomes.[3]

3. See, for example, Barrett, *Cognitive Science Religion and Theology*; Brown and Strawn, *The Physical Nature of the Christian Life*; Clarke, *All in the Mind?*; Jeeves and Brown, *Neuroscience Psychology and Religion*; and McNamara, *The Neuroscience of Religious Experience*.

3

At the heart of this rather prodigious project lies the grounding and sustaining element of the Christian faith. Its inspiration has blossomed from God's acts of compassion all throughout the ages without fail and is calling us to restore compassion at the center of our faith life. The resources that we have at our disposal to accomplish this task are immense and the grain of truth scattered in various disciplines and wisdom traditions are there for us to discern and distill. As we answer this call and set out on a journey that will have us traverse various paths, we hold on to the intimate knowledge of God who is our anchor and guide and whose incarnation in Jesus Christ offers a compelling portrait of compassionate presence.

Lest we get lost in the realm of ideas, this book aims at couching the discussion in an experience-near fashion. Life is replete with human interest stories of suffering and compassionate acts, some of which will be infused into the narrative with great care and sensitivity. These are stories of real people both near and far and whose identity will remain hidden to protect their privacy. Some of these are our own experiences; others are culled from our experience of life both in the domains of personal and professional. Our vocations as professors, psychotherapists, and pastors of local congregations have afforded us an intimate look into lives of our students, clients, and fellow believers. Their life stories have intersected with ours and have made us better clinicians, caring workers in the vineyard of God, and ultimately simply persons questing to incarnate God's compassion in the little corner of the world we live in. In line with this personal touch, a significant portion of the book is devoted to a detailed discussion of compassion cultivation practices that individuals and groups may want to use as part of their spiritual disciplines or personal and communal formation. After all, this book is conceived first and foremost as a practical guide to a more compassionate life rooted within the framework and narrative of the Christian tradition.

The Roadmap of the Journey

Now that the general contour of the book has been laid out, we can proceed with a thorough description of its components, starting with a brief definition of compassion. Compassion is an innate human disposition that is evoked within us when confronted with suffering and fuels our desire to alleviate and transform it. As we know, compassion plays a central role in the teachings of all world religions. Christianity, in particular, authenticates itself and demonstrates its vitality through compassionate engagement with those suffering. Such commitment to "suffer with" is deeply grounded in Jesus Christ, who serves as its paradigm and source of motive power. Compassion is a visible expression of God's solidarity with and intimate regard for the welfare of humanity, which is punctuated by the incarnation of Jesus Christ.

Sadly, sustained acts of compassion most often recede into the background and discourse on beliefs is increasingly occupying the center stage. In a way, "wanting to be right" or "being right" supplants "doing right" from its pivotal place as the true measure of a living, vibrant, and diffusive faith. The issue here is not the content of belief and more about the manner in which such belief is held—usually inflexibly, insistently, and idolatrously. And as history so clearly has shown us, this has resulted in indifference and disengagement with the world Christians are supposed to serve. Even worse, this obsession towards "wanting or being right" has spawned various forms of violence, abuse, and cruelty directed at those who do not share the same beliefs. The name of God is used to justify these horrific acts.

The main purpose of this book is to reclaim compassion as the pulsating heartbeat of the Christian life. Three related questions serve as a framework for the ensuing discussion, to wit:

1. What role does compassion play in God's economy given the unremitting and ubiquitous nature of human suffering? The religious character of compassion can be described as God's radical response to human suffering. Jesus incarnate and his compassionate heart is God's answer to the cries of the vulnerable, marginalized, and displaced.

2. What are the cognitive and affective underpinnings as well as the physiological and neurological correlates of compassion? The scientific approach taken here highlights the subjective and bodily experience of compassion by carefully delineating its psychological roots and biological markers gleaned from evolutionary psychology and brain science.

3. How might compassion cultivation training nurture and nourish the trait of compassion? What effects might this training have on individuals who stand in the gap or mediate God's compassionate presence amidst a hurting world? The ethical dimension of compassion hinges on mirroring a Christlike character trait of compassion and the nurturance and promotion of pro-social and altruistic behaviors.

These overarching questions are given full treatment in subsequent chapters briefly described below. Chapter 1 deals primarily with the issue of human suffering, which is such a powerful trigger for compassionate response. This issue has already captivated the minds of many—in fact, a slew of books and articles have already been written about it. And rightly so, since the experience of suffering is so immediate, direct, and devastatingly disorienting it demands a theological response. For our purposes, we argue that a compassionate response, at least from a Christian world view, is closely linked to a biblical and theological understanding of human suffering, which this chapter endeavors to expound.

Chapter 2 delves deeply into a particular kind of human suffering that is actually preventable yet so achingly pervasive. It is also a clear distortion of the Christian message. This form of suffering we are talking about is violence and cruelty committed against those considered in the "out-group." Too often, the name of God is used to justify or legitimize this violence.

Chapter 3 makes a hopeful turn and encouraging tone given the nature of the preceding two chapters. The theme of compassion is discussed here more fully from the different yet complementary hermeneutical perspectives of biblical theology, psychology, and brain science. This layered analysis hopes to provide a nuanced and comprehensive approach to compassion that is lacking in current literature. The parable of the Good Samaritan (Luke 10:25–37) and Jesus' Feeding of the Five Thousand (Mark 6:30–44) occupy a central place in this section and they are used as a paradigmatic example of what it means to be compassionate.

Chapter 4 ventures into the role of the mind in initiating, nurturing, and sustaining a life of compassion. This section entails a basic description of the mind and brain and their relationship to each other and delineation of brain areas that mediate the experience of compassion. It also explores how compassion cultivation practices can facilitate changes in the brain (neuroplasticity), and by extension change the person's way of being in the world as well. The foregoing eventuates into an analysis of what it means to have the "mind of Christ" or "the renewing of the mind" and then integrate this with insights gained from brain science.

Chapter 5 translates knowledge extracted from the previous chapters into practical wisdom. This takes the form of a series of interrelated and sequential spiritual exercises that will help nurture and sustain a life of compassion. They complement and support other spiritual disciplines, and are simple and accessible to everyone desiring to partake of the opportunity to grow the seed of compassion. It begins with an exercise called "Mindful Heart and Mind," which is a general introduction to the practice of mindfulness and contemplation as a necessary ingredient to the cultivation of compassion. This is followed by the exercise called "The Compassionate Heart of God" aimed at remembering and receiving God's manifold acts of compassion, which finds its ultimate expression in the incarnation of Jesus Christ. The personal experience of God's compassion through Christ quickens a movement towards self-empathy and compassion—the major focus of "Self-Compassion."

Chapter 6 hones in on extending compassion to others. The first of this series of exercises is called "Compassion For a Loved One" and is designed for someone dear and close to us who is going through a time of pain and suffering. It then moves into the exercise "Compassion for a Neighbor" that brings to mind and heart someone we know (e.g., a friend, fellow believer, co-worker, client, or the like) whose life situation engenders a need for compassion. Having built a stronger foundation and commitment to a life compassion we can now enter into an exercise that is meant for someone whom we differ or have conflict with, and may consider an enemy or threat. The goal of this exercise, called "Compassion for a Challenging Other," is to go beyond differences and into an acknowledgement of their personhood and our commonality with them as fellow human beings on a journey. The last of this series is a practice called "Compassion for All," which as the title implies is about extending compassion to all sentient beings near and far.

These spiritual exercises, though arranged sequentially, can be practiced separately depending on the need of the moment and the unique circumstance of the person. However, it would be best to start in the order in which they are arranged and let oneself be fully immersed in the process and its pattern and then later on select which exercise fits best given a situation at hand. Additionally, we have designed the book in such a flexible way it can be translated or used as a workshop topic or Bible study theme or book study for small groups or classroom use.

Compassionate Presence

As professors, psychotherapists, and parishioners we have seen the many faces of suffering. As human beings we have also been pierced by the rough edges of our own doing and the fallen world we inhabit. Yet in the midst of all that the presence of a compassionate God remains constant—sustaining, healing, transforming, and reassuring. Though this presence sometimes eludes our conscious awareness and is difficult to discern the fact remains—God's faithful companionship never fails.

In a lavish display of the grace and companionship of God, this compassionate presence often takes on the face of ordinary people whose accompaniment during these dark times is marked by mindful attention, empathic attunement, and a loving desire to relieve such suffering without imposition or intrusion. This commitment to "suffer with another" through concrete acts of mercy and human solidarity incarnates God's compassionate heart in a profoundly personal and compelling manner. Such theological assertion springs from an experiential knowledge of God who in love became flesh and suffered with and on our behalf and who calls us to offer that love and compassion to ourselves and those around us. Isn't that central to our identity? Isn't that what we are here for? That is, to be a people of God bound by love, transformed by love, and compelled to show this love to all without conditions and limits; to offer hospitality to the displaced and different; to stand alongside victims of injustice and inhumane practices; and to awaken those hypnotized by materialism, religious fundamentalism, and self-ism. Indeed, the call to compassionate love is urgent yet immense. However, this is not ours to own and we cannot willfully do it without the agency of God moving in, around, and through us. Our role primarily is to ready ourselves to the task. This little book shows a way to do just that.

Chapter One

Compassion and Suffering

It was Friday morning, November 8, 2013, when news about the devastating and life-negating effects of Typhoon Haiyan in Tacloban, Philippines reached the comfort of our homes in Canada. Images of a city reduced to rubble of shattered dwellings and dreams, lifeless bodies and displaced survivors, flattened infrastructures and concerned rescuers splashed on our TV screen. Chaos blanketed the city and suffering of all kinds is etched on the faces of those who survived Haiyan. We sat in our living room aghast at what we saw and simultaneously grieved with the Filipinos whose lives were turned upside down by nature's wrath. Immediately after the typhoon had waned, we learned of the overflowing display of kindness and support that came flooding from all over the world to help survivors rebuild their lives anew.

Sophia, a fifty-five-year-old woman, walked into her therapist's office visibly distraught and defeated. Her face looked haggard and her voice started to quiver as she narrated her marital woes. Her husband of thirty years carried on an affair with his co-worker for almost a year, she confessed with great sadness and pain. Burdened with raging and conflicting emotions, she launched into a litany of questions and gestures that revealed a heart that was wounded and shattered into pieces. Her sense of confidence as a woman and lover was shaken and the future of their marriage now uncertain. Sophia's cry of anguish and desperation has evoked a need for gentle therapeutic accompaniment and compassionate response in her therapist.

The news about the gruesome murder of Tina Fontaine, a fifteen-year-old teenager from the Sagkeeg First Nation, and the brutal sexual assault of sixteen-year-old Rinelle Harper in the fall of 2014 have cast a glaring spotlight on the persistent problem of racism in Winnipeg and Canada as a whole. The violence committed against these two young aboriginal women and the continuing onslaught of racist comments hurled at First Nations people reveal the depth of intolerance and racism embedded in the collective psyche of this supposedly progressive and inclusive country. Yet against this dark and gloomy backdrop was a beacon of light in the form of a community coming together at a vigil to show its support and declare its commitment to work against all forms of racism and discrimination.

These are just a few stories of suffering that are eerily familiar and evocative, and come to us with disconcerting regularity. The sight and sound of individuals in excruciating pain contained in these stories break through the armor of illusory separation and break open an intense desire to help, to intervene, and to make a difference. Compassion is its name and it is triggered when we bear witness to the suffering of another. This response is at the heart of Christianity. It is rooted in the incarnation of Christ, which made visible the depth of God's love, solidarity, and intimate regard for humanity. It is also part of who we are as beings created in the image of God who is full of compassion and love.

The religious character of compassion opens up a way of addressing the issue of human suffering, which leads the question of the sovereignty and goodness of God. Why is there so much suffering in the world? If God is love, good, and powerful, why does God let suffering continue? These burning questions are often raised by many a Christian who tries to make sense of the ubiquitous and debilitating nature of suffering in their lives. And sadly, the answers often given are full of platitudes or guilt-inducing or run-on statements in defense of God.

What follows is neither an attempt to explain suffering away nor will it try to quickly justify suffering as a means to some higher and loftier end. Instead, this theological reflection endeavors to identify the cause of suffering and the unique role that compassion play in addressing this problem. Before we proceed, though, it is important to say at this juncture that we are mindful of the limits of words in describing, let alone easing, the pain and suffering of another. However, we hope that this theological excursus will help illumine and inform the path of compassion we all are called to take and inspire us to come alongside people who are desperately looking to find meaning out of the chaos and disorientation that suffering brings. In this journey of faithful companionship, concrete acts of compassion are usually coupled with and most acutely experienced when offered in comforting silence, coupled with quiet reassurance that sufferers are not alone in this painful process. At least, this has been our own experience when providing accompaniment in therapy and also when on the receiving end of this same gesture of concern from others.

Suffering and the Problem of Evil

One cannot really talk about suffering without touching on the age-old problem of evil that many a theologian, biblical scholar, and philosopher has grappled with over the centuries. Evil and human suffering cross paths in dire situations and they often leave a scar no balm can quickly soothe. Yet, no matter how intertwined they are, a distinction needs to be made between human suffering and the problem of evil to avoid collapsing these realities into one and the same thing—e.g., suffering *as* evil.

We begin by addressing the problem of evil. Augustine of Hippo (354–430 AD), an early Christian theologian and philosopher, claims that evil is the corruption or rejection of good. It does not exist in its own right, like there is an evil force dueling it out with a benevolent entity for dominion and supremacy, but instead is "parasitic on something good."[1] Of course, this does not really explain why evil exists in the first place. Instead, it refutes the dualistic idea that there are "two equally ultimate principles behind good and evil" which "makes it more and more difficult to affirm equally ultimate powers independent of God, thus compromising his omnipotence."[2] Simply put, a doctrine of God's sovereignty precludes the presence of another malevolent force that exists apart from God and that can threaten God's sovereignty over all creation (Isa 45:6–7).

Human suffering is the exact opposite of good. We are not talking about the good or value that may come out of suffering, though that is certainly possible and consequential at times. We are talking about the physical and mental suffering that evil, as a corruption of good, brings about. In most cases this corruption is engineered by human beings whose propensity to tarnish and taint the good is awfully rampant and often unbridled. But as we know, that is not the only cause of human suffering that we see around us. Equally ominous and intractable is the suffering inflicted by forces of nature that can claim thousand of lives in an instant. As we can see, human beings are besieged either by the choices of others or

1. "Augustine on Evil"
2. Hebblethwaite, *Evil, Suffering and Religion*, 44–45.

11

themselves (moral evil) and the seemingly capricious nature of the natural world (natural evil). Regardless of the source, though, the impact remains the same—human beings suffer greatly often beyond what they can bear— and the need for a compassionate response remains urgent.

Human suffering can be traced back partly to the moral evil that pervades reality. By *moral evil* we mean the "wickedness of human beings . . . this is, evil that is seen in things that are said and done, things that are perpetrated, caused, exploited, by human action or inaction."[3] The story of Sophia vivifies what this means in concrete terms. Her husband has willfully strayed from his commitment to remain faithful to her by engaging in an extramarital affair with his co-worker. This has resulted in marital discord that led to a temporary separation immediately after he was confronted. The psychological impact this had on Sophia was so severe she needed to undergo weekly therapy sessions. She was deeply hurt and was tormented by images of her husband in bed with another woman. She had lost confidence in herself as a person and lover and started to blame herself for her husband's indiscretion. Her defeated demeanor, bouts of crying, and debilitating fear of losing her marriage pervaded her time in therapy. In this story, we see that the good inherent in the marriage is now corrupted by someone's wayward choice.

On a larger scale we are also assaulted everyday by horrifying news of suffering wreaked by human beings whose moral compasses have gone awry, are fractured, or are seemingly nonexistent at times, in the case of antisocial behavior. Take the case of the two teenagers in Winnipeg who suffered horribly, even fatally for one of them, because of their gender and ethnicity. The blood that courses through their veins made them easy targets for perpetual racism and discrimination, leaving them feeling unsafe, profiled, and violated in their own land. There are countless other stories of this nature from other people of different ethnic or racial backgrounds. The good that is inherent in cultural and racial diversity is corrupted by a distorted view that sameness needs to be upheld and defended and difference is a threat that needs to be avoided or punished.

The picture gets worse when we turn our eyes to the history of the Christian church, which is replete with stories of unspeakable acts often executed either in the name of God or by those who claim to be followers of God. In fact, strands of the contemporary church continue to be implicated in numerous accounts of religious violence and cruelty committed against

3. Wright, *The God I Don't Understand*, 30.

those who fall outside or in opposition to their truth claims. Often the commitment to dogma results in some being excluded or ostracized, and even seriously harmed or violated. We will look at this expression of moral evil more closely in Chapter 2.

A close reading of passages such as Psalm 5:6; Isaiah 31:2; Micah 2:1; Job 34:10; 2 Samuel 10:12; Mark 10:18; and Luke 18:19 offers a radically different picture of God[4] than those held by individuals whose actions contribute to evil and suffering in the world. Unfortunately, the message of God's compassion and God's call to be compassionate to all recede into the background. What tends to take center stage and therefore accorded with utmost importance is dogma or "right belief" as opposed to doing what is right.

From a theological standpoint moral evil ultimately links back to humanity's continuing rebellion against God or the perversion of will that is turned against God.[5] It is God who sets the parameters of what is good— "Love the Lord your God with all your heart and with all your soul and with all your strength and with all your mind"; and, "Love your neighbor as yourself" (Deut 10:12; Luke 10:27). When human beings assert themselves against the revealed will of God (Exod 20:3–11; Deut 5:7–15; Matt 22:37–40; Mark 12:30; Luke 10:27), or when love of self is cut off from the love of God and love of neighbor, evil and suffering inevitably ensues. But what has instigated this desire to overthrow God from God's rightful place and put self in the throne instead?

Here lies the difference between moral evil and sin nature. Sin can be described in two ways—factual and actual. We all are born into a state of rebellion, alienation, and estrangement from God (Rom 3:23) and therefore vulnerable to betraying and rejecting God's will and intentions for our lives. This sinful nature gets actualized through the moral evil we commit against each other, personally and corporately conceived. Moral evil "finds its roots in the disobedience, whether deliberate or accidental, premeditated or unpremeditated . . . to the will of God, and as such becomes associated with generic sin and virtually synonymous with wickedness."[6] This wickedness yields fruits of suffering that hems us in from all sides. Thankfully, we can be freed from the shackles of sin that enslaves us (Rom 6:6) and therefore need not suffer in perpetuity. God's radical response to

4. Elwell, ed., *Dictionary of Biblical Theology*, 219.

5. Hebblethwaite, *Evil, Suffering and Religion*, 57.

6. Elwell, ed., *Dictionary of Biblical Theology*, 222.

this is an outpouring of unconditional love and compassion embodied in the incarnation, suffering, death, and resurrection of Christ (Rom 5:8, 15) who in turn calls his followers to love without limits or conditions and to show compassion to all (Eph 4:32, Phil 2:1, Col 3:12, 1 Pet 3:8).

The other category of evil is called *natural evil*, which renders most, if not all, of its victims feeble and paralyzed at its sheer power and seeming randomness. It can strike anywhere anytime, often without warning. It does not discriminate and it brings in its wake excruciating pain and suffering at the loss of lives, properties, identities, and meaning that cannot be linked or referenced to human will.[7] The tsunami that hit Thailand in 2004, the magnitude nine earthquake which then unleashed a tsunami in Japan in 2011, and Typhoon Haiyan that made landfall in the Philippines in 2013 are devastating examples of the unpredictable and often fatal properties of the natural world. The scope of devastation and the senseless deaths of many elicit a cry of protest—"Why does God allow such horrific suffering?"—so loud it renders us bereft of speech but not without any means to alleviate it.

There is another kind of suffering that feels justified and necessary at times. Suffering as divine punishment, testing, and discipline is perhaps the most common form of suffering that is "peculiar to God's people."[8] It is peculiar because it's purposeful, that is, the suffering that God metes out transforms God's children in myriad ways as shown in such passages as Hebrews 12:5–12:

> In your struggle against sin you have not resisted to the point of shedding your blood. And have you completely forgotten this word of encouragement that addresses you as children? It says, "My son, do not make light of the Lord's discipline, and do not lose heart when he rebukes you, because the Lord disciplines those he loves, and he chastens everyone he accepts as his child." Endure hardships as discipline; God is treating you as his children. For what children are not disciplined by their father? If you are not disciplined—and everyone undergoes discipline—then you are not legitimate children at all. Moreover, we have all had parents who disciplined us and we respected them for it. How much more should we submit to the Father of spirits and live! Our parents disciplined us for a little while as they thought best; but God disciplines us for our good, that we may share in his holiness. No

---

7. Hebblethwaite, *Evil, Suffering and Religion*, 52.

8. Carson, *How Long, O Lord*, 64.

discipline seems pleasant at the time, but painful. Later on, however, it produces a harvest of righteousness and peace for those
who have been trained by it. Therefore strengthen your feeble
arms and weak knees.

God's discipline is meant to help followers of Christ to: 1) combat sin (v. 4);
2) see it as an expression of God's love and as a source of encouragement to
those who desire genuinely to please the Father (v. 5–9); 3) recognize that
it is for our own good and as a way of sharing in his holiness (v. 10), hence
we are called to persevere, endure suffering, and not give up; 4) take it as
an identity-affirming experience of our status as God's children (v. 8); 5)
accept that it will hurt and to rest in the assurance that those who embrace
God's discipline with endurance will yield fruits of righteousness and peace
(v. 11).[9] Instances where God disciplines his children are plentiful—from
being engulfed by plagues and illnesses to personal losses to outright punishment and rebuke—and its effect always painful.

And then there is Job, whose suffering seems undeserved and incom-
prehensible. In the story, we witness "irrational evil, incoherent suffering"[10]
descend upon Job who has been described as "blameless and upright, a
man who fears God and shuns evil" (Job 1:8; cf. 1:2; 2:3). As the stories
goes, Job, stupefied by what has befallen him, laid bare his heart in protest
(Job 30:16–21).

> And now my life ebbs away; days of suffering grip me.
> Night pierces my bones; my gnawing pains never rest. In his great
> power God becomes like clothing to me; he binds me like the neck
> of my garment. He throws me into the mud, and I am reduced to
> dust and ashes. "I cry out to you, God, but you do not answer; I
> stand up, but you merely look at me. You turn on me ruthlessly;
> with the might of your hand you attack me."

Here is a man questioning, lamenting, and protesting not God's power but
God's justice in a profound, penetrating, and deeply personal way. Yet, his
protests seem to have fallen on deaf ears. God seems out of reach, detached
and unmoved by his cry of anguish and tormented soul. There is only silence and Job is left to bathe in his own tears of sorrow and pain. God's
silence appears less mysterious and more malicious, it seems.

Then his friends came along with the intention to provide comfort
and accompaniment. For a while they sat with him without uttering any

9. Ibid., 64–66.
10. Ibid., 136.

words, muted perhaps by the depths of Job's suffering. But as we later find out, that is short-lived for they hastily made a case that his suffering was evidence of guilt. Expectedly, this only fuels Job's indignation towards God and his "despair becomes an emotional indictment of God, blaming God with indifference—if not hostility—to the unjust suffering of innocent beings"[11] like him.

Unbeknownst to Job, there is actually a backstory behind this and a message that is difficult to decipher. According to the narrative, his suffering came about as a result of a transaction happening elsewhere between God and Satan. God has granted Satan permission to inflict Job with misfortunes, intolerable suffering, and incalculable losses—the point of which was hidden from him.

Towards the end of the narrative (Job 38–42), still no encouragement or explanation was given. Instead, we encounter a litany of questions and pronouncements that only "highlights the hidden character of God's wisdom in the world,"[12] a wisdom that Job needs to grapple with on his own and must surrender. This submission came in the form of repentance for "his arrogance in impugning God's justice,"[13] and unbelief in God's sovereignty and goodness. But as the story reaches its climax we witness God restoring Job beyond measure not as a reward so as to affirm the doctrine of retribution, nor was it a recompense for his faithfulness under extreme testing. This restoration was offered simply as a gift.

Job's innocent and meaningless suffering discloses that there "remain some mysteries to suffering . . . to exercise faith in the God who graciously revealed himself to us"[14] in love and compassion. This foreboding sense of ambiguity inherent in the suffering that we sometimes experience lures us to stand on the promise of God's quiet accompaniment holding us together as we are lurched to and fro by the storms of life (1 Cor 10:13).

It also encourages us to take a radical step beyond doubt and unbelief and to throw ourselves unreservedly into the loving embrace of a compassionate God "who appears when God has disappeared in the anxiety of doubt."[15] God breaks through the veil of our suffering and offers his grace and promise of compassionate companionship.

11. Beker, *Suffering and Hope*, 38.
12. Ibid., 39.
13. Carson, *How Long, O Lord*, 153.
14. Ibid.
15. Tillich, *The Courage To Be*, 190.

To sum up our discussion so far, human suffering emerges from a host of sources—from the choices that we or other people make (moral evil) to the suffering induced by natural disasters (natural evil). It can also be inflicted as God's way of disciplining us or as a result of God's own choosing whose reasoning and meaning may elude us. Yet amidst all this we are not left unaided or abandoned. God knows the suffering that people bear to the extent that he intentionally enters into the "structures of his creation [to bear] the brunt of the world's evil himself to the point of crucifixion."[16] That is compassion in action driven by God's great love for humanity and embodied more fully in the person of Jesus Christ. The dark shadow of suffering is kissed with the light of God's compassion.

Suffering and the Body of Christ

God, who is *apart from* (transcendence) and *a part of* (immanence) the world he created, is active and intimately involved in shaping human history to move towards a particular desired end.[17] Realized historically through the incarnation of Jesus Christ, the "pivot of human history, the central point of revelation and redemption,"[18] this movement involves "the gradual fashioning of a world of persons, whose perfection will be realized only in ultimate future"[19] when the Lord Almighty reigns (Rev 19:5–7). We come in hopeful anticipation that when he returns in glory this promised perfection entails that all suffering will finally come to an end.

> He will wipe away every tear from their eyes. There will be no more death or mourning or crying or pain, for the order of things has passed away. He who was seated on the throne said, "I am making everything new." (Rev 31:4–5)

Integral to this salvation history is the active calling and fashioning of a people from disparate backgrounds and constituting them to be the body of Christ as a "vehicle of God's special providence in the world."[20] The church mediates God's providence through concrete acts of mercy, justice, and

---

16. Ibid., 67.

17. Hebblethwaite, *Evil, Suffering and Religion*, 85.

18. Ibid., 86.

19. Ibid., 54.

20. Ibid.

Inanition towards

compassion, which subverts the negating power of sin and offers people hope, healing, and transformation.

To keep this calling fresh for the church, the gift of the Lord's Supper is enjoined a confessional proclamation—Christ has died! Christ is risen! Christ will come again! This liturgical acclamation is a way of bringing into the present moment the manifold benefits and cosmic significance of the passion, death, resurrection, and the coming of the Lord Jesus Christ.

When we enter into and participate in this communal celebration we acknowledge with deep gratitude and thanksgiving God's display of unconditional love for us all. Compassion emerges from this vast, expansive, and inclusive love of God. God knows our human predicament—the power of sin that destroys, distorts, and deceives and the suffering it brings—and out of his love and compassion has reached out from the heavens, became flesh and dwelt among us, and gave his life for us.

> He was despised and rejected by mankind, a man of suffering, and familiar with pain. Like one from whom people hide their faces he was despised, and we held him in low esteem. Surely, he took our pain and bore our suffering, yet we considered him punished by God, stricken by him, and afflicted. But he was pierced for our transgressions, he was crushed for our iniquities; the punishment that brought us peace was on him and by his wounds we are healed. We all, like sheep have gone astray, each of us turned to our own way; and the Lord has laid on him the iniquity of us all. (Isa 53:3–6)

This is the ultimate expression of God's compassion, symbolized compellingly in the breaking of the bread and the drinking of the cup. The word "compassion" means to "suffer with," which is taken from Latin word *com* (or together) and *pati* (to suffer). The verses just considered describe in great detail the extent to which Jesus Christ, the Suffering Servant, showed his compassion. He took upon himself "our pain and bore our suffering, he was pierced for our transgression and crushed for our iniquities" (vv. 4–5), and through this he brought comfort and hope by trumping and triumphing over sin and death and being offered as new life (2 Cor 5:17; Rom 6:4). The bread represents Christ's body broken for the world and the cup his blood spilled in sacrifice on our behalf. These religious symbolisms make concrete and visible God's self-giving love, revealed profoundly in the incarnation of Christ (John 3:16), the object of ritual worship and paradigmatic example of compassion.

The gathered community around the table provides the impetus for members of the body of Christ to commune with each other in the name of their Lord. Sharing in one loaf and drinking from the common cup rallies the people of God in all times and all places in all levels of social, economic, and political life (Matt 5:23ff; 1 Cor 10:16ff; 1 Cor 11:20–22; Gal 3:8) to promote "justice, truth, and unity" as well as "human personality and dignity."[21] For this to happen, the church needs to be "broken" itself in the sense of putting away its selfish ambitions, prejudices, and differences and offering itself in the service of others. Doing so, it shows compassion for those in the throes of suffering, darkness, and defeat.

This message is captured fully in the Apostle Paul's account of the Lord's Supper. Paul's narrative places this celebratory meal within the context of betrayal and disunity in the church at Corinth. The Lord's sacrificial death, his body and the cup given as the new covenant, has reconciled humanity to God, and humanity to itself (Rom 5:10). Ironically, this message of reconciliation has eluded the church Paul addressed, which evidenced selfishness and divisiveness in its communal gathering, an act that rendered it "guilty of profaning the body and blood of the Lord" (1 Cor 11:27).

Instead of breaking bread together as one body of Christ, these Christians allowed themselves to be ruled by their own prejudices and social status, and lacking in compassion they neglected the poor amongst them. The aim of the narrative then is to help the Corinthian church regain its perspective on what the ritual represents to it as the newly constituted Body of Christ.

> For I received from the Lord what I also passed on to you: The Lord Jesus, on the night he was betrayed, took the bread, and when he had given thanks, he broke it and said, "This is my body, which is for you: do this in remembrance of me. The same way, after supper he took the cup, saying, "This cup is the new covenant in my blood; do this in remembrance of me." For whenever you eat this bread and drink this cup, you proclaim the Lord's death until he comes. (1 Cor 11:23–26)

Through the Lord's sacrificial death humanity is no longer at enmity with God, and through that restored relationship, God gave them the ministry of reconciliation (2 Cor 5:18) and admonished them to have compassion (Eph 4:32; Phil 2:1; 1 Pet 3:8). In turn, the Lord's Supper must be celebrated in a manner that reflects the spirit of sharing and unity in Christian life

21. *World Council of Churches Faith and Order Paper No. 111,*14.

and faith until he comes again. Reminiscent of the promise in Revelation 31:4–5, the Lord's Supper is also a foreshadowing of a heavenly banquet, which is a "scriptural picture for the enjoyment of salvation in terms of communion with the Lord"[22] that includes an experience of shalom or completeness, peace, harmony, and absence of discord, suffering, and pain.

The contemporary church, sad to say, continues to struggle with the same issue that the Corinthian church suffered from. In fact, it is actually getting worse in that the call for reconciliation and compassion recedes further and further into the background and war over doctrinal issues takes center stage, leaving a trail of division, emotional scars, spiritual abuse, cruelty, and religious violence in its wake. Right belief has become paramount over and against treating persons rightly—as someone who bears the image of God and whom God came and died for—almost to the point of idolatry. When this happens the church fails to fulfill its iconic function and image as a vehicle of God's special providence in the world.

How might we understand this growing fracture that is threatening the spiritual integrity and calling of the Christian church to be the body of Christ "broken and given" to the world as a sign of God's compassionate love to all of humanity? How might we explain the shift away from "treating persons rightly" as the true expression of the religious life to an obsessive emphasis on having the "right belief" that often yields cruelty and religious violence towards those in the "out-group"? These are the questions we will endeavor to explore in the next chapter.

---

22. Marshall, *Last Supper and Lord's Supper*, 153.

Chapter Two

Compassion and the Other

The sound of praise to God Almighty reverberates within the walls of our church. With eyes closed and arms lifted up we sing poignant songs of love that is unconditional, forgiving, and inspiring. Our lips utter words that build us up and bind us together as one under the lordship of the triune God. The joint singing creates a sense of communion—one with the other, and with God. In that hour our shared belief in and expression of worship to God takes center stage. Our differences, whether in personalities, appearances, emotional styles, or faith journeys, fade away, at least momentarily. What remains, at least in the realm of the external, is a concerted effort to focus one's attention on the object of worship—God. This, of course, is stating the obvious. We see such expression of worship in most, if not all, Christian churches around the world.

So far so good, right? Well, not quite! Alarmingly, the lips that proclaim God's love for all, at least in certain strands of Christianity, may also be the same lips that dish out words of disapproval, contempt, and dismissal towards those who do not share their beliefs around such hot-button issues as homosexuality, women in leadership roles, and divorce—to name a few. Hard lines are drawn and almost instantaneously people are bracketed into two contentious groupings: the "in-group" or those who adhere to a more conservative or fundamentalist stance towards these issues, and the "out-group" or those who see no conflict between these issues and their Christian faith. Admittedly, the dynamics involved in setting boundaries between the two groups are far more nuanced, complicated, and reciprocal. However, having the *right belief* as opposed to *treating others rightly*—with compassion, curiosity, respect, and dignity—takes primacy and seems to be *the* acceptable form of admission into the fold. Those who fall outside the boundary are seen as a threat that must be converted or won over, guarded or fought against. This "circle the wagon" approach literally creates an out-group, and many on the inside have little to no comprehension as to how this impacts those on the outside. Those on the inside have a particular logic; that in order to protect right belief, the out-group needs to be isolated and contained. Further, in order for the out-group to gain access, the out-group needs to adapt, which leads to having little appreciation for how alienating being on the outside is and leads to confusion and indignation. The actions taken towards the out-group can be quite cruel and in some ways violent, but this is typically not recognized as such by those on the inside.

This compels us to ask: how can the interior ground of the heart yield both fruits of heartfelt praise to God and thorny thistles of exclusion and alienation towards those who bear the same image of God as us? What follows is an analysis, albeit provisional, of this confounding question using the hermeneutical perspectives of evolutionary psychology and brain science. But why this route, one may ask? The answer is simple, really, if we come to think of it. Spiritual stirrings and religious beliefs and commitments do not float in the air detached from the body that feels, thinks, and behaves. In other words, our spiritual act of worship and the beliefs that we hold about God and other divine matters are grounded in our body and are concrete and localized expressions of a brain and mind created to adapt to the environment around it. Hence, the question posed early on does not only require a theological response. It also calls for an analysis that looks deeper into its biological and psychological underpinnings.

Ultimately, the goal of this chapter is not only to expand our horizon of understanding with regards to this pressing concern. It is about practicality as well. That is, it is about exploring various ways of subverting this "two-faced tendency" by nurturing and enlivening our capacity for empathy and compassion for all utilizing insights and resources gleaned from these allied disciplines.

The Development of the Moral Brain

At its core, evolutionary psychology considers that "behavior, belief, emotions, thinking and feelings are all functions of a fully embodied brain. As the brain is a physical organ, it, like all other physical organs, has an evolutionary history . . . the product of evolutionary process that shaped this organ in response to environmental selection pressures."[1] Over a long period of time, the brain has gradually evolved into a "collection of task-oriented and problem-solving mental tools"[2] as a way of navigating a challenging, unpredictable, and ancient environment. To many evolutionary psychologists, this specialized and instinctual neural wiring is etched deeply into the brain and has left an indelible mark on contemporary behavioral and cognitive patterns, which are now being revealed with such fascinating detail by cognitive sciences.[3]

With this discovery we can now approach the religious mind and explore our propensity to produce in one seamless and uninterrupted movement the most profound spiritual insights and the most horrendous ideations and acts of cruelty and religious violence against others. More particularly, what triggers the neural activation of this ancient brain system that propels deeply committed believers to act with such intention against those that hold different and divergent views? How might religious beliefs induce and condone inhumane treatment of others? And how have we come to hold such beliefs that run contrary to the message of love and compassion that is central to Christianity in the first place?

Acknowledging the strain of violence embedded in the deepest level of religious imagination,[4] however disconcerting this might be, is a good place to start. This is in no way desacralizing our religious tradition. It only exposes this strain that "flows naturally from the moral logic inherent in many religious systems" including Christianity, and is "grounded in our evolved psychology."[5] But what does this mean? More precisely, what is the nature of this moral logic that is capable of producing both religious morality and religious violence?

In its basic form, morality is concerned with "judgments about right and wrong, good or bad, as these terms are used to judge interpersonal relations."[6] According to cognitive scientific study these judgments are instinctual and often the result of "intuitive, emotionally based reactions to

---

1. Teehan, *In the Name of God*, 2.
2. Ibid.
3. Ibid.
4. Juergensmeyer, *Terror in the Mind of God*, 6.
5. Teehan, *In the Name of God*, 147.
6. Ibid., 15.

social interactions,"[7] which are then given rational justifications.[8] In other words, morality is not solely the domain of reason as often claimed by moral philosophers, nor is it simply a prescribed list of behaviors generated from the Scriptures. Numerous functional magnetic resonance imaging (fMRI) studies reveal a much more complex scenario where both emotion and cognition are implicated in the process of making moral judgments.[9] Hence, when faced with moral dilemmas human beings make quick and instinctual responses that emanate "below the horizon of consciousness" and are caused by a complex network of "neurally based cognitive and affective systems."[10] This innate moral grammar that lies outside of conscious awareness and powerfully influences moral judgments is believed to have evolutionary origins. That is, it evolved out of necessity to meet the "demands faced by individuals pursuing their reproductive fitness"[11] amidst a socially demanding and challenging environment. It is comprised of such elements as kin selection, reciprocal altruism, indirect reciprocity, among others, and is emotionally charged and powerful in navigating and shaping human interactions.[12] Over time, this moral grammar developed into a coherent moral system that is found in all cultures.

> If a society is to function at a level beyond the clan it must develop a system to effectively encourage and reward cooperation, and to discourage and punish defectors and cheats. This is what moral systems are designed to do: to establish a code of behavior that promotes and rewards behavior necessary to cohesive social functioning, while condemning and punishing behavior contrary to cohesive social functioning . . . . To the extent that a moral code taps into this evolved moral sense it gains great intuitive and emotional appeal. It can move people to act because it triggers the cognitive and emotional predispositions that generate behavior.[13]

Religion, being one of the most enduring and powerful cultural institutions, is a potent force in promoting group cohesion. Through the lens of evolutionary psychology, religion is able to achieve such a feat by "regulating

7. Ibid., 16.
8. Ibid.
9. Green, "Emotional engagement in moral judgment."
10. Teehan, *In the Name of God*, 19.
11. Ibid., 41.
12. Ibid.
13. Ibid., 42.

human behaviors in a pro-social manner by triggering evolved cognitive/emotional mechanisms."[14] Of course, religion extends its reach and function beyond the promotion of social cohesion and identity. We take seriously its encompassing power and longevity in bringing about spiritual transformation and transcendent meaning in the lives of its adherents. We are acutely aware of this and we acknowledge religion's multifaceted dimensions and purposes.

As religion codifies behavior through a series of moral imperatives it divides people into two groups with distinguishable codes and ethics—the in-group, or those who adhere to its moral codes, and the out-group, or the outsiders who are less, if at all, invested and committed to the group. Social cohesion is established within a group by promoting pro-social behavior marked by reciprocation among members of the group.[15] However, this social expectation has a dim outcome. It is exclusionary in nature in that if you don't belong to a clan "then you are an outsider . . . hav[ing] less motivation to cooperate or to reciprocate cooperation and, therefore may pose a danger to the community. For all the constructive morality found in religion, we find an equally prominent place for warnings against outsiders."[16] Being excluded is not only a marker, at its worst; it merits an unwanted and sometimes injurious or fatal consequences. For this to happen the out-group is not only excluded, they are also "otherized,"[17] subjected to various forms of cruelty and violence.

The otherization of certain individuals or groups is infused by an overestimation of self and the degradation of others because they adhere to a belief that is different and contrary to the established norm and values of the in-group.[18] Worse, the out-group is then further otherized by attributing to them what is called the "essence trap."[19] Here, their misdeeds or ill-conceived choices are considered to be reflections of their flawed nature, their character or essence. Consequently, a clear demarcation is drawn by emphasizing their difference from the in-group, "pushing the unpleasantness away to a more comfortable psychological distance and pushing the

14. Ibid.
15. Ibid., 148.
16. Ibid.
17. Taylor, *Cruelty*, 8.
18. Ibid.
19. Ibid., 9.

person away with it . . . purely because we have beliefs about other people which lead us to push them into hated outgroups."[20]

Such is the power of belief! It has the capacity of constituting disparate individuals into a group with a shared identity and purpose that is derived from their commitment to a belief system. The flip side of this is disconcerting because this same belief system can also be used as a justification to exclude others to the point of dehumanizing them simply for not making the same signal of commitment.

Beliefs gain their strength when delivered and heard repeatedly, causing stronger synaptic connections and neural patterning in the brain to occur.[21] To be more specific, "this strengthening tends to happen when the neurons they connect are repeatedly co-activated. This may occur when one neuron triggers the second, or when other signals trigger both at once."[22] No wonder it is extremely difficult to give up or change beliefs that have long been held dearly, because neurologically they are intricately embedded or sculpted in the brain's neural networks. Likewise, beliefs also gain a foothold when they induce fierce and clear patterns of neural activity that fit nicely with neural patterns already in place and comes with an "emotional boosters to help carve their impression into cortex."[23] They are also likely to produce unwavering commitment when these accepted beliefs are uncomplicated, consistent, and easy to understand and decisively support the personal and communal narrative and identity of their followers.[24]

This anatomy of belief, albeit brief, provides the necessary conditions for otherization to happen. Messages delivered may be varied and casually rendered yet in its basic form they propagate a very clear and simple story with three overarching beliefs—"people are different, disgusting, not like you; these people want to harm you or have already harmed you or people like you; removing these people will solve your problems."[25] These core messages are couched in familiar and compelling stories and in a language that fits the context of their listeners. The effect of such skillful otherization is alarmingly predictable in that these key ideas ease more gently and

20. Ibid.
21. Ibid., 149.
22. Ibid.
23. Ibid.
24. Ibid.
25. Ibid.

deeply into the brain especially when paired with an effective use of strong emotions to back up their claims.[26]

One such emotion is disgust. Disgusting stimuli evoke a powerful combination of physical and behavioral reactions—from changes in breathing and distinct facial expression to nausea and vomiting.[27] These aversive reactions to disgusting stimuli are innate or pre-programmed so as to allow for "early detection and avoidance of disgust-threats."[28] They have also evolved as a way of protection from perceived or actual threat.[29] Triggers include food, body products, sex, animals, interpersonal contamination, and moral offense, among others.[30] When confronted by these triggers people walk away in haste without much thought or provocation.

On a neuronal level, these reactions are complex, automatic, fast, and highly choreographed, involving the stomach, the vagus nerve, and the brainstem, among others, to elicit a disgust response. Otherization relies on the repetition of the core message of difference and the accompanying emotion of disgust that one should feel towards the outsiders. The more disgusted we feel about the person or group the greater avoidance tactic is assumed. The disgust response can even go as far as eliminating the source of this aversive reaction.

As said previously, a signal of commitment and reciprocal cooperation are important elements of social cohesion. Any deviation from this incurs exclusion, particularly when beliefs, ideas, or views are divergent and incompatible with what the in-group holds to be true. To justify the otherization of the out-group, the in-group relabels these ideas to make them appear more dangerous and threatening. The metaphor of ideas as pathogens and infectious succeed in eliciting countermeasures to block the out-group's ideas from spreading.[31] In effect, what they are really saying is that "people who have wrong ideas are plague-being organisms and ought to be eliminated for the sake of public health."[32] Not only are the ideas dangerous, but the people who hold them are disgusting and therefore must be kept at bay and avoided at all cost. Thus, the chasm between the in-

26. Ibid., 150.
27. Ibid., 131.
28. Ibid.
29. Kazen, *Emotions in Biblical Law,* 93.
30. Ibid.
31. Taylor, *Cruelty,* 158.
32. Ibid., 149.

group and out-group widens and the animosity between the two groups is intensified.

Empathic Brain

Individuals who are always on high alert to mitigate actual or perceived threat are in danger themselves. The chronic activation of the stress-threat response can damage the body and can pose undue risk in matters of interpersonal relations. The latter takes the form of deficits in the empathy quotient.

Empathy is the ability to inhabit the world of another to gain a fuller understanding of and appreciation for their thoughts and feelings and ways of being in the world. It is nonjudgmental, sensitive, open, curious, and hospitable to the uniqueness of the person's internal world without losing one's own. It fosters genuineness, respect, honesty, and vulnerability in human relationships. Through it, minds meet and hearts commune in unity without sacrificing each other's differences and singularity. It promotes pro-social behavior, reciprocity, and cooperation, which help facilitate the growth and flourishing of human society. In fact, the human species is a rich reservoir of empathy by virtue of our shared experiences as human beings. Our commonality far outweighs our differences, which makes empathy readily accessible and available (in the absence of pathology).

And out of this fertile ground the seed of compassion grows and can bear much fruit. Born out of empathy, compassion sees the suffering of another and vows to alleviate it in a non-intrusive and non-threatening manner.

Empathy is mediated by "mirror neurons" or brain cells that light up when we watch someone perform an action (e.g., moving a hand) and then having the inkling to do the same and understand their intentions.[33] This "motor empathy" is intertwined with cognitive empathy or theory of mind (i.e., the ability to infer thoughts, beliefs, and perspectives based on the behaviors of others) and affective empathy (i.e., the ability to detect the feeling of another). These three coalesce together to form a wonderfully orchestrated manner of social engagement that rely on the "fundamental statistical facts of brain function: the correlations which ensure that similar events, on the whole, produce similar neural patterns."[34]

33. Vittorio, "Action recognition in the premotor cortex."
34. Taylor, *Cruelty*, 180.

To be more exact, these psychological events occur in the right hemisphere of the brain.[35] The ability to see the interconnection of things, curiosity, interest and identification with others, self-awareness, and empathy are largely dependent on right hemisphere resources.[36] Particularly, when we try to put ourselves in the shoes of another, "we are using the right inferior parietal lobe, and the right lateral prefrontal cortex, which is involved in inhibiting the automatic tendency to espouse one's own point of it."[37] This means that the activation of this section of the brain makes possible the openness to divergent views and the willingness to be convinced of positions that have not been previously supported.[38]

In a broader sense, the right hemisphere has great affinity when it comes to emotional receptivity and expressiveness.[39] It is faster than the left hemisphere at detecting facial expression of emotion, reading subtle information that comes from the eyes, and understanding the emotional subtext of language.[40] It also plays a crucial role in animating the face and the prosody or intonation of voice to express emotions.[41] This is not to say though that the left hemisphere has no part in the understanding and expression of emotion. The difference lies in the fact that the left hemisphere is more involved in the conscious representation of emotion, whereas the right hemisphere is more directly involved in the immediate—even unconscious—reception, expression, and processing of emotion.[42]

The hemispheric difference between the right and left side of the brain becomes starker when it comes to attention. In this context, attention is much more than a mental function alongside reasoning, memory, and acquisition of information.

> The kind of attention we bring to bear on the world changes the nature of the world we attend to . . . . Attention changes what kind of a thing comes into being for us: in that way it changes the world . . . . Attention also changes who we are, we who are doing the attending. Through the direction and nature of our attention, we

35. McGilchrist, *The Master and His Emissary*, 57.
36. Ibid.
37. Ibid.
38. Ibid.
39. Ibid., 58.
40. Ibid., 59.
41. Ibid., 61.
42. Ibid., 62.

prove to ourselves to be partners in creation, both of the world and of ourselves. In keeping with this, attention is inescapably bound up with value. Values enter through the way in which those functions are exercised: they can be used in different ways for different purposes to different ends.[43]

The right hemisphere sees the world more as a whole; it prioritizes context and the interrelatedness of things and people, and attends more acutely to the bigger picture.[44] The left hemisphere has a more focused and narrower attention, it sees mostly the individual parts and not the whole, and attends with much precision.[45] Both hemispheres function differently out of necessity. Together they need to bring to bear two incompatible types of attention on the world at the same time, one narrow, focused, and directed by our needs, and the other broad, open, and directed towards others.[46] This has ensured our survival and eventual success in navigating this complex and challenging world to our own benefit and advantage.

Though the two hemispheres differ in what they attend to, the right hemisphere does not have to know what the left hemisphere knows for that would compromise its ability to have the big picture view.[47] Neither should the left hemisphere be privy to the activities of the right hemisphere because "from inside its own system, from its point of view, what it believes it has created appears complete."[48] Here lies its weakness, especially if the knowledge gained is not reintegrated back to the right hemisphere, which provides a complete and panoramic vista and more socially meaningful information about the self and the world.

The value of the left hemisphere is making the implicit explicit, "but this is a staging post, an intermediate level of the processing of experience, never the starting point or end point, never the deepest or the final level."[49] Unfortunately, the left hemisphere has become its own master instead of an emissary.[50] A world that is dominated by the left hemisphere is described as mechanical, abstract, disembodied, distanced from feelings, pragmatic,

43. Ibid., 28.
44. Ibid., 27.
45. Ibid.
46. Ibid.
47. Ibid., 207.
48. Ibid.
49. Ibid., 209.
50. Ibid., 428

overconfident of its own view on reality, and lacking insight into its problems.[51] It is primed for competition and power[52] and when it forgets its function and place in light of the whole it offers a world that is stunningly familiar to what we have now. The current Western zeitgeist privileges rationality and empirical evidence as the only legitimate source of truth. It craves power and control and encourages abstraction and detachment from feelings, relationships, and community, which leaves us more isolated, disconnected, and divisive than ever before.

Empathic Failure

Consequently, this left hemisphere bias dampens the ability to form meaningful bonds with others. The empathy circuit, which is largely a function of the right hemisphere, is turned off, so to speak. As a result, this failure to make empathic connection makes otherization inevitable, especially in cases where the line between who is in and who is out has already been drawn. The left hemisphere can be coopted to serve the purpose of otherization. Its narrow and limited focus can render members of the out-group purely as threats or objects to be avoided or eliminated and not appreciated as persons just like them—with feelings, families, and foibles. Its penchant for power and competition can be redressed as a way of justifying the all-too-consuming desire to win at all costs, even if that may mean taking the life of another. Its propensity to privilege reason or a particular way of reasoning can be coopted or manipulated to rationalize various forms of cruelty and violence, believing that somehow they are deserving of such horrific acts because they exercise self-agency and dance to the beat of a different drummer. The tie that can bind one to another is cut off such that the pain and suffering displayed by those who are otherized is obscured. The in-group is indifferent and unaffected by the suffering of their counterpart. They can be deaf to their cries of anguish and blind to their harrowing plight.

These empathic failures are not only expressed behaviorally through acts of avoidance, indifference, and non-response towards the suffering of the out-group. The brain reflects or captures these behavioral responses as well in fine detail, as revealed through various fMRI studies.[53] For example, in a recent study of racial bias it is revealed that the "out-group members—

51. Ibid.
52. Ibid.
53. Avananti et al., "Racial bias."

merely by virtue of who they are and not anything they have done—reliably elicit diminished perceptions of suffering and fail to elicit equivalent physiological and affective empathic responses. More concerning is that these dampened empathic responses are related to less helping."[54] This is quite disconcerting and yet so true and rampant in today's society. And as we know otherization goes beyond differences in race. Its tentacles reach even further to include those who fall outside of the mythical norm (middle class, male, able bodied, educated, married) and the tactic to widen this gap remains the same—from avoidance to expulsion to elimination.

A Perfect Storm

> In evangelical Christianity, the Bible is perfect, it is God's word and it must be adhered [to] strictly. So there is this expectation set on you, this goal that is set that you have to live by these certain criteria. And if you don't do that you are not one of us, and if you are not one of us you are probably going to hell because we believe it's true . . . and only what we believe is true.[55]

Darren Freeman uttered these poignant words with sadness and pained look on his face in the documentary film *Cure for Love*. For most of his youth, Darren struggled mightily to reconcile his "same-sex desires" with his faith as an evangelical Christian. He tried to deny it for fear of going to hell, a message he heard repeatedly from the pulpit. From that same platform, he also heard gays stereotypically portrayed as promiscuous men, which confounded him greatly as he was not sexually active. This internal conflict and unremitting messages of judgment and condemnation threw him into despair and loneliness. John Holm, another guy featured in the film, has internalized this homophobia that resulted in self-hate and self-mutilation. He resorted to "razors, steak knives, and meat scissors" to ease the pain of a "profound sense of shame for his life and how God found him disgusting." At one point, he planned to castrate himself and to overdose on antipsychotic drugs, as he could no longer deal with the torture of being torn apart by the split between himself, God, and his sexuality.

Sadly, stories like these are far too common, with endings so predictably devastating. The process of otherization so sharply delineated by

54. Cikara et al., "Us and Them."
55. *Cure for Love.*

Darren's testimony taps into this ancient brain circuitry that sets off an in-group–versus–out-group mentality. Boundaries are then rigidly drawn and those that fall outside are dehumanized and devalued. Their humanity is stripped of any dignity and respect. The image of God in them is dismissed and denied. They are treated with disdain and judged as disgusting, an abomination before God, unnatural, and ungodly. Such hateful messages aroused vigilance to protect the in-group from interpersonal contamination and moral offense defensively through avoidance and/or offensively through expulsion or extermination (e.g., hate crimes).

But what creates the condition where the strain of cruelty and violence embedded in the religious mind comes alive and active? For one, religious belief plays a pivotal role in quickening this strain to action. In a survey done in the US in October 2003 by the Pew Research Center for The People and The Press and the Pew Forum on Religion and Public Life, it is revealed that many "Americans remain highly critical of homosexuals and that religious belief is a major factor in these attitudes."[56] In general, homosexuality remains a major topic in churches and other places of worship and is frequently addressed by the clergy from the pulpit.[57] A more telling result indicates that:

> The clergy in evangelical churches focus considerably more attention on homosexuality and address it far more negatively than do ministers and priests in other denominations. Two-thirds of evangelical Protestants who attend church services at least once a month say their ministers speak out on homosexual issues, compared with only about half of Catholics (49%) and just a third of mainline Protestants (33%). And compared with others who attend services where homosexuality is discussed, substantially more evangelicals (86%) say the message they are receiving is that homosexuality should be discouraged, not accepted.[58]

Fast forward to June 2015, when another survey was conducted by Pew just weeks before the US Supreme Court made the ruling that the US Constitution guarantees a right to same-sex marriage. Results indicate that support for same-sex marriage is at an all-time high (57 percent) and 39 percent oppose. Compare that to five years ago where more opposed same-sex

---

56. Pew Research Center, "Religious Beliefs Underpin Opposition to Homosexuality."

57. Ibid.

58. Ibid.

marriage (48 percent) than supported it (42 percent).[59] Indeed, the tide has changed, at least in some quarters of the American populace. In the religious sector, particularly among evangelical Christians, the picture remains the same. That is, religious belief still figures prominently in the discussion.

> One of the strongest factors underlying views of same-sex marriage is religion, and the sense that homosexuality is in conflict with one's religious beliefs. White evangelical Protestants stand out for their deep opposition to same-sex marriage: Just 27% favor allowing gays and lesbians to marry, while 70% oppose it (43% *strongly* oppose); by contrast, majorities of both Catholics (56%) and white mainline Protestants (62%) support same-sex marriage, along with an overwhelming majority (85%) of the religiously unaffiliated. And among the one-third (33%) of Americans who feel there is a lot of conflict between their religious beliefs and homosexuality, opposition to same-sex marriage outweighs support by more than two-to-one (70% oppose, 27% favor).[60]

Differences in belief are inevitable and even warranted, especially if the pursuit of truth is the focal point of theological discourse. Unfortunately this pursuit is often obscured or coopted by an insatiable desire to be right. Hence, when the quest for truth takes the back seat and is replaced by the quest for certainty, power, and control, theological discourse becomes a platform to silence, denigrate, and label those with opposing and alternative views as disgust-threats. Nowhere is this more evident than the issue of homosexuality and the Christian faith, at least among certain strands of Christianity.

Several factors conspire together to produce implicit and explicit homophobic attitudes that are so prevalent among conservative evangelical Christians. First of these is the incessant litany of negative preaching about homosexuality by the clergy from their pulpit. The result of the survey mentioned above attests to this alarming fixture of the group's ethos. When this type of preaching is combined with a strong emotional tone of disapproval and disgust it creates a sense of righteous indignation especially when backed up by scriptural claims. But unbeknownst to many preachers and hearers, this exchange gets etched deeper and deeper into the brain networks causing them to react almost instantaneously in a predictable manner. The threat system of the brain is activated and defensive

---

59. Pew Research Center, "Support for Same-Sex Marriage Record High"

60. Ibid.

or offensive posture is taken. Rigid lines are once again drawn, commitment to the in-group's moral code enforced, and the out-group otherized through various forms of cruelty and violence—all in the name of religion. Invoking the name of God to justify acts of cruelty and violence is the most pernicious form of spiritual abuse. To make matters more complex, many times there is a corresponding belief that the in-group is reaching out in love and not in hatred, often evidencing the lack of awareness of the impact of such rigid lines.

The documentary film *For the Bible Tells Me So* captures this troubling reality vividly. The films follows the lives of five young people whose relationships with God and their families were disrupted and challenged when they realized that they were gay. Some of the commentaries made by priests, rabbis, pastors, and theologians in the documentary, in fact, allude to this process of otherization. For example, Rabbi Brian Zachary Mayer comments, "the cheapest way of getting the feeling that we are a group or a family or something is to make an other and it's throughout history with different groups . . . civil rights with the blacks and anti-Semitism with Jews to have an other. And homosexuals, unfortunately, are the new other."[61] As startling as this may sound, there remain attempts to coopt the Bible to further one's personal, theological, even political agenda, just like in the past where it was used to justify racism, slavery, subjugation of women, and persecution of Jews.[62]

Secondly, preaching (and teaching for that matter) tends to favor left-brain–mode processing. The structured nature of sermons delivered from the pulpit appeal to the left hemisphere's way of organizing information—logical, linear, focused, and representational. Repeated activation of this mode of processing caused by repeated negative preaching on homosexuality yields a strengthening of synaptic connections or neural activity in this part of the brain (neurons that fire together wire together, as the saying goes).[63] Consequently, since most preaching on homosexuality is also peppered with negative emotional subtext, a stronger impression into the cortex is carved or sculpted.[64] The more hearers strongly believe the message they receive from the pulpit the more certain they can be that the

61. *For the Bible Tells Me So.*

62. Ibid. See also Taylor, *Cruelty,* and Teehan, *In the Name of God.*

63. Taylor, *Cruelty,* 149.

64. Ibid.

message is true.[65] Otherization relies heavily on this type of communication exchange and neuronal activation.

With the narrow outlook and grasping or needing-to-take-control tendency of the left hemisphere comes a detached, overconfident, and emotionally inaccessible and unavailable relational stance with self and the world. The over-activation of the left hemisphere dampens the activation of the right-brain mode processing, which is integral in seeing and making connections, showing interest in and identification with others, and manifesting self-awareness and empathy.[66] This reduced capacity to show empathy is the third variable that underpins the otherization of gays and lesbians. During the confirmation of Gene Robinson, an openly gay clergy, as Bishop of New Hampshire by the Anglican Church in 2003, a slew of scathing letters came pouring in. Injurious and abusive remarks like "I hope that someone stones this faggot to death," "you fornicating lecherous pig," "if you had any courage you would kill yourself like all queers," "the Holy Bible is the road to heaven and God says death to the faggots" littered these letters.[67] Such verbal abuse can only come from individuals whose ability to empathize and to see other people as people bearing the image of God is greatly impaired. They are blinded by their own self-righteousness and oblivious or unmoved by the pain and suffering they brought upon those whom they consider as threats and enemies. All these factors create a perfect storm that drowns the dignity and worth of those otherized into the abyss of dehumanization.

Calming the Storm

But this storm can be quieted down and our brain is equipped or has evolved to fulfill this task. Just as the process of otherization triggers the threat system in the brain so can the soothing and affiliative system[68] be activated through the induction and promotion of empathy and compassion. This is corroborated by neuroscientists and evolutionary biologists who claim that the "innate biology of the human brain compels us to be

65. Ibid., 145.
66. McGilchrist, *The Master and His Emissary,* 57.
67. *For the Bible Tells Me So.*
68. Gilbert and Choden, *Mindful Compassion,* 63.

kind. That is, we are wired for goodwill . . . . In this context the word goodness has lately become associated with notions of empathy."[69]

What a great reminder this is especially in a time when armed conflicts
rule the streets and hog the headlines, when culture wars and the perpetu-
ation of otherization and isms (e.g., racism, sexism) are institutionalized
and practiced in the name of religion. The flicker of goodness cannot be
distinguished despite the overwhelming evidence to the contrary. This is
no longer just a philosophical or theological assertion but a real scientific
proof borne out of laboratories and field work.[70]

Altruistic Brain Theory (ABT) represents this emerging work that ex-
plains in detail "how the brain produces altruistic behavior"[71] and through
that can help "change how real people organize their lives."[72] The five-step
theory details concrete steps our brains take to engender altruistic behaviors, which occur outside of our conscious awareness. The process is sum-
marily delineated below.

Step 1: Representation of what the person is about to do. The central
nervous system registers the act that is about to be performed by the benefactor toward another person. The same nerve cells at the top of the neural
system that will command the muscles to contract (and hence undertake
the act) also send a second, identical message back to the sensory system
of the brain that essentially says "these muscles are about to contract in this
manner."

Step 2: Perception of the individual toward whom the benefactor will
act. When the actual beneficiary is right in front of the benefactor, the patterns of light, dark, and color that pass through the eye of the actor (the
person who is about to behave, i.e., the benefactor) cause electrical signals
to be sent from the cells of the retina; the signals travel through the optic
nerve. The signals follow two major pathways. The simpler, more primitive
pathway heads for the midbrain, where visual signals can be put together
with signals from other senses to get a rapid picture of what is in front
of the actor and enable rapid, almost automatic action. The longer, more
detailed visual pathway special to the human brain travels to the very top
of the brainstem; a signal travels here to the very back of the cerebral cortex, the visual cortex. There, individual features of the image of the other

69. Pfaff, *The Altruistic Brain*, 5.

70. Ibid., 22.

71. Ibid., 7

72. Ibid., 8.

person—lines, angles, shadows—converge in-group of cells to form a unified image.

Step 2 is crucial to ABT because we cannot act toward another human being unless we can literally picture that person—or visualize a generic person—in all of his or her humanity. This is part of the communal impulse, necessary for our survival and as such part of God's creative design.

Step 3: Merge image of the other with self. This step is crucial, as it provides the basis for treating the other person like oneself. How? The answer is: an increase in the excitability of cortical neurons, such that when the nerve cells representing the other are firing signals, the nerve cells are representing self are also firing. There are three cellular mechanisms that can do this. One is that inhibition in the cortex is reduced. A second mechanism is that tiny tunnels between nerve cells are created, thus allowing electrical excitations to spread quickly. A third mechanism implicates excitation by the powerful neurotransmitter acetycholine. In addition to these three mechanisms for merging sensory images of other with self, the so-called mirror neurons unite the actions of another person with our own.

Step 4: Activation of the altruistic brain. The representation of the act (Step 1) and the united, combined image (from Step 3) must arrive at an "ethical switch" in the brain just before we carry out an act toward another person. As a result, instead of literally seeing the consequences of the act for another person, we automatically envision the consequences as pertaining to our own self. While this ethical evaluation may occur at a conscious level, it also can be instantaneous and unconscious. This takes place primarily in part of the brain that is bigger and stronger in the human brain than in other brains: the prefrontal cortex. There, a value—"good" or "bad," "do" or "don't do"—is attached to the combination of the act and combined self/other target. These prefrontal cortical neurons allow the positive, altruistic act to proceed.

Step 5: Performance of an altruistic act. The output from the prefrontal cortex permits the motor cortex and subcortical movement control neurons to perform the act that was so rapidly and automatically evaluated. Step 5 is necessary to turn an ethical decision by neurons in the frontal cortex into an actual behavior.[73]

We have all heard stories that testify to the goodness of humanity—from daily random acts of kindness to heroic deeds of ordinary people (e.g., 911 first responders) to concrete expression of human solidarity towards

73. Ibid., 55–63.

those afflicted by natural disasters (e.g., relief aid for victims of Typhoon Haiyan). That these acts of altruism are mediated by the human brain that has evolved throughout human history make this scientific discovery all the more significant in the way we orient and order our lives. That is, to tap into this innate capacity in the service of those who suffer and to participate in their human flourishing. But these mechanisms have to be harnessed and nurtured with intentionality and regularity because they can "provide the basis for new initiatives that clear away the impediments to pro-social behavior and allow people to perform on a regular basis in accordance with their potential."[74] The latter point will be expounded more fully and concretely in subsequent chapters.

The science behind altruism, which can address and mitigate the challenges posed by otherization, complements in such a beautiful and compelling way the very heartbeat of the Christian message—extending God's unconditional love and compassion to all human beings. The "stuff" or the brain mechanisms needed for this to happen is intricately wired in every fiber of our being. It is in our DNA, so to speak. It is part of God's design for us, a way of mirroring or reflecting the very image of God who is love and is full of mercy and compassion. Somehow and for some reason this calling has taken the back seat. But with the resource provided by brain science we can begin to infuse new insight into the meaning of Christ's admonition to his disciples to "love one another." With love that is enfleshed in empathy and compassion, altruism's key elements, we can begin to chip away at the barrier of otherization we have built around us and create spaces where hospitality of the other reigns supreme.

What might this look like in practice? For example, how might we calm the perfect but devastating storm of otherization of gays and lesbians using the Altruistic Brain Theory (ABT)? Applying the five-step theory of ABT to this case may look something like this.

Step 1: Representation of what the person is about to do. For this to happen, the congregation needs to create an atmosphere of hospitality by preaching messages not of contempt or condemnation but of understanding and compassion towards the suffering of gays and lesbians who have been the target of otherization.

Step 2: Perception of the person toward whom the benefactor will act. This means putting a face on the issue and hearing others' stories, which may subvert every stereotype and negative sentiments to which the

74. Ibid.

congregation has been exposed in the past. It will also pave the way for people in the church to encounter a real person behind the label whose humanity may touch their own, thus evincing empathy and compassion towards their struggles. When paired with a message of Jesus' unconditional acceptance, especially towards those marginalized by society, it will trigger activity not only in the left hemisphere of the brain but in the right hemisphere as well, thus inducing empathy and identification with them as fellow human beings in need of God's grace, mercy, and compassion. The focus here lies in an acknowledgement of the person's humanity without judgment and conditions, as someone who bears the image of God and for whom Christ died unreservedly. This atmosphere of hospitality plants a seed of empathy that can yield fruits of compassion and altruism.

Step 3: Merge image of the other with self. Evoking empathy through face-to-face and right brain to right brain interaction between the two groups will make it easier for the congregation to enter and inhabit the difficult and challenging world of those otherized because of their sexuality. Hopefully, this will provide a much deeper and richer understanding of their situation and the suffering they have to endure every single day of their lives. The firing of cortical and mirror neurons in the brain as they merge the image of the other as God's dearly beloved to their own self-understanding as God's image bearer will bridge the gap that has long been created by the fear, ignorance, and indifference. In this process of merging humanity's essential nature as compassionate altruistic beings who are wired for connection and communion is valued and will begin to emerge as their defining core identity.

Step 4: Activation of the altruistic brain. The preceding steps result in a cascade of neural firings that will trigger an activation of the altruistic brain that perhaps has been muted or dampened by an over-activation of the threat system during the process of otherization. Turning the pre-frontal cortex or the "ethical switch" of the brain online, as it were, will inspire and energize an act of altruism based on an experience of shared humanity. Stretching the arms wide open to receive the personhood of the other is also a way of championing the ethic of reciprocity contained in the Golden Rule—"Do to others as you would have them do to you" (Luke 6:31).

Step 5: Performance of the altruistic act. Showing empathy and compassion towards the other is an important and concrete first step in alleviating the suffering of those otherized and seeing them as persons and objects of God's love. As this seed is planted and nourished in the life of the congregation they will become more aware, reflective, and critical of their actions and advocate for a just, respectful, and humane treatment of their fellow human being who happens to be gay or lesbian.

There are several things that must be articulated here before continuing. First, we are acutely aware of the complexity surrounding this issue. Notice that the focus of the discussion is on developing an authentic, non-threatening, and compassionate stance and relationship with the other by tapping into our altruistic brain and not on doctrinal issues that have often divided people and fractured relationships. This is by design, as we would like to give primacy to relationship that is based on mutual respect and trust since we believe that only when this is established can we truly enter into meaningful dialogue with one another. Second, the application of ABT is not specific to the otherization of gays and lesbians. It can also be applied to any group that has been marginalized and otherized by society in general and church in particular (e.g. LGBTQIA, women, ethnic and racial groups, Jews, Muslims, etc.). Third, we recognize how deeply ingrained these prejudices are and how intractable the pain and suffering this has caused others. The neatly arranged five-step model of ABT is not meant to streamline a reality that is so layered with personal, societal, and religious subtexts. It is appropriated to shed light on the biological underpinnings of altruism and to remind us that we are hardwired for connection, communion, and compassion.

Since experience has the capacity to alter both the structure and function of the brain what sorts of conditions and experiences might help facilitate the activation of the altruistic brain in a sustained and habit-forming manner and limit those impulses that undermine such proclivities? Put another way, how might we transform our mind to be empathic and compassionate towards those who suffer? What practices might help nourish and sustain a life of compassion? We now turn to these pressing questions, starting with an exploration of the nature of compassion from an integrative perspective of theology and brain science.

Chapter Three

The Face of Compassion

We have heard the story before, perhaps countless times. A man was robbed and was left for dead on the side of the street. Stripped of his dignity and belongings he laid there wounded, alone, and half dead (Luke 10:30), perhaps groaning in pain and pleading for help. This appalling scene could evoke pity so overwhelming it would cause anyone witnessing this dire situation to act hurriedly to save this man. Anyone? Well, not really, according to the parable in Luke 10:25–37.

FIGURE 1. Vincent van Gogh (1853–90), *The Good Samaritan* (after Delacroix), 1890. Oil on canvas. Rijksmuseum Kroller-Muller, Otterlo, Netherlands.

The first witness to this event was a priest who "saw" the ailing man but chose to look the other way and "passed by on the other side" (v. 31). Faced with suffering he responded in a manner that seems incongruent with who he is and what he stands for. Then another temple representative came, a Levite this time around, travelling on the same road. He "saw" the wounded man. Unmoved by this sight, he, too, looked the other way and "passed by on the other side" (v. 32). Here's another religious man who seems to have betrayed or ignored the essence and call of a religious duty. Two passersby came and went but the situation remained the same. The man who was robbed still lay there fighting for dear life.

Vincent van Gogh, inspired by Delacroix, captured the first few but critical moments in the parable in the painting of the same name (see Figure 1). Notice that the first two characters are barely visible; the priest dressed in a brown garb is some distance away from the scene, choosing a different path, that of convenience and apathy for the plight of the suffering man. The Levite, also wearing the same brownish cloak, is not far behind with his back turned against the man dying, and his head lowered with him reading a book. Like the priest, he too showed indifference and neglect, and chose to live in his own self-possessed world unmindful of the suffering and tragedy around him. The priestly garb and the book, most likely the Torah, is emblematic of his role and identity as a mediator of God's presence, yet all that melted away into oblivion. Van Gogh's use of dull and muted colors that blend seamlessly into the background reveal the inner life of these two characters—void of vibrancy and congruence.[1]

Then the "Good Samaritan" arrived on the scene and he did the unthinkable. He, too, "saw" the man, but unlike the priest and the Levite, he "took pity on him" (v. 33). Filled with compassion the Samaritan "went to him, bandaged his wounds, pouring on oil and wine. He put the man on his own donkey, brought him to the inn and took care of him" (v. 34). Yes, the Samaritan made himself available to this man through his undivided attention, caring presence, and sharing of resources to ensure the healing and well-being of this wounded man. Here is compassion displayed in the concreteness of the Samaritan's engaged response and action.

In the painting we see the Samaritan and the wounded man front and center. Their bodies are intertwined or joined together, a vivid image of empathy, compassion, and identification with the man's pain and suffering. His back is slightly arched and with force and intensity he lifts the bruised

---

1. Resseguie, *Narrative Criticism of the New Testament*, 27.

man onto his donkey. The vivid depiction of the Samaritan's heartfelt response to suffering is juxtaposed against the cold, detached, and heartless response of the priest and the Levite. Van Gogh's painting captures this contrasting attitude and disposition. The dull color donned by the priest and the Levite pales in comparison to the Samaritan's vibrant red headgear, bright golden cloak, and brilliant blue tunic, which the Samaritan shared with the man to cover his nakedness. In these strokes of contrasting colors van Gogh conveys the presence of "life and hope in the midst of tragedy."[2] The evocative power of the parable lies in its central character—the Good Samaritan—whose status in society has been recast in a fresh and radical manner.

The words "good" and "Samaritan" are an interesting combination given the explosive tension between Jews and Samaritan during the time of Jesus.[3] And yet in this parable, Jesus used a despised foreigner, a Samaritan, to be an exemplar of compassion or neighborly love. After binding his wounds with oil and wine he lifts him with all his might and "places him on his own beast. The priest is the one who sacrifices animals. The Samaritan uses the animal to help. The Levite was the one trained in the law, theoretically the law of love: The Samaritan is the one who lives out the law of love."[4]

This motif of reversal in the parable, which renders the "despised Samaritan the hero and the Bible-believing and obeying priest and Levite the villain"[5] is framed within the context of an interesting exchange between an expert in Jewish law and Jesus (v. 25). "What must I do to inherit eternal life?" asked the lawyer. The intent of his questioning seems dubious and deliberately designed to "test" Jesus, to "draw out from him a teaching suggesting that one can inherit eternal life while bypassing the Law."[6] In a Socratic fashion and perhaps sensing the lawyer's hidden motive, Jesus replied with a question of his own. "What is written in the Law? How do you read it?" (v. 26). Not to be outwitted, of course, the lawyer retorted by citing the great commandment from Deuteronomy 6:5: "Love the Lord your God with all your heart, with all your soul, with all your strength and with all your mind," and Leviticus 19:18, "Love your neighbor as yourself" (v. 27). This is the heart of Jewish law and both Jesus and the lawyer knew that.

2. Ibid., 28.

3. Byrne, *The Hospitality of God*, 100.

4. Dornisch, *A Woman Reads the Gospel of Luke*, 134.

5. Nadella, *Dialogue Not Dogma*, 72.

6. Byrne, *The Hospitality of God*, 99.

Satisfied with the lawyer's answer, he admonished him to translate the heart of this law into a life lived in love and he would inherit eternal life (v. 28).

But the lawyer is unrelenting. Unnerved by the simple yet profound answer of Jesus and wanting "to stay focused on codifying his deeds of love"[7] he asked "and who is my neighbor?" (v. 29). As someone who is well-versed in Torah and therefore acquainted with its many laws requiring Israelites to show mercy to everyone without limits and conditions this question brims with prejudice and hidden agenda. The question "Who is my neighbor?" is his way of "asking Jesus to interpret the Torah as to the kinds of people Jesus would exclude from his love,"[8] those people outside of the "covenantal community of Israel . . . sinners who were ignorant of the Law, and any other outsiders, particularly Gentiles."[9]

Much to his dismay, Jesus answered not with a straightforward statement but with a story of the Good Samaritan that turns his Pharisaic world upside down. As the unlikely hero of the story, the despised Samaritan, who does not have the law per se but fulfills it wholeheartedly through his concrete acts of mercy and compassion, has become the epitome of what it truly means to love one's neighbor as oneself.

After telling the story, Jesus re-engaged the lawyer with a very simple yet direct question. "Which of these three do you think was a neighbor to the man who fell into the hands of robbers?" (v. 36), to which he replied, "the one who had mercy on him," (v. 37). Stretching the lawyer beyond the confines of merely knowing the Torah, he admonished him to "go and do likewise" (v. 38). He is now faced with a challenge, that is, "he is to cease and desist his legal maneuverings to avoid the central issue. God, as revealed in the Torah, and especially as revealed in Jesus, is a God of love, mercy, and compassion. Jesus calls the lawyer to show love and mercy as a converted man to whom God's mercy has come—in the Torah and now in Jesus."[10]

Compassion as Neighborly Love in Action

The story of the Good Samaritan is a story of neighborly love that is scandalous in its inclusivity, outrageous in its display of concern, and radical in its generosity. To what extent does the face of compassion as revealed in

7 Just, *Concordia Commentary*, 451.

8. Ibid., 452.

9. Ibid.

10. Ibid., 454.

the story of the Good Samaritan echo the way compassion is understood in the ancient Greco-Roman world to later Jewish, New Testament, and early Christian writings? A short excursion into the evolution of this word as used during those times is offered below.

As a noun, the Greek word *splanchnisomai* originally means "the inward parts of a body, including especially the viscera"[11] or internal organs or gut, which is put aside and then eaten at the start of the sacrificial meal.[12] It also means the "lower part of the body, especially the womb and loins" that connotes the "seat of the power of procreation."[13] Eventually though, the term evolved to mean "the heart . . . the center of personal feeling and sensibility or tenderness" and was construed as "a more blunt, forceful, and unequivocal term."[14]

One wonders if the "bodily based" understanding of compassion helps describe our physical reaction when witnessing someone in pain and the subsequent welling up of tenderhearted intention but forceful desire to help alleviate the suffering of another. This word origin bears a striking connection and relevance to the current discussion of the science of compassion, as we will discuss later on.

Later Jewish writings carried this understanding of compassion with a particular emphasis or weight heaped on its emotional and volitional quality. These writings render compassion as a "positive stirring of pity . . . higher will, conviction, sympathy . . . a guiding inner disposition that leads to loving mercy"[15] towards those who suffer.

In the Old Testament, compassion is definitively an attribute of God (Exod 34:6, "The Lord, the Lord, the compassionate and gracious God"), showered freely (Exod. 33:19) like a parent caring graciously and tenderly for a child (Isa. 49:15; Hos 11:8). God's compassionate nature is intimately tied to God's covenantal relationship with God's people (2 Kings 13:23, "But the Lord was gracious to them and had compassion and showed concern for them because of his covenant with Abraham, Isaac, and Jacob. To this day he has been unwilling to destroy them or banish them from his presence," for which they render praise). This is also reflected in Psalm 78:38, "Yet he was merciful; he forgave their iniquities and did not destroy them.

11. Danker, ed., *A Greek Lexicon of the NT*, 548.
12. Ibid.
13. Ibid.
14. Ibid.
15. Ibid., 549.

Time after time he restrained his anger and did not stir up his full wrath." Finally, it is declared that compassion comes after wrath (Jer 12:15), is new every morning (Lam 3:22–23), and conquers sin (Ps 51:1).[16]

The New Testament usage of compassion takes a different yet complementary route. The verb form of the word is strictly found in the synoptic Gospels. Outside of the parables (Matt 18:23–35; Luke 15:11–32; Luke 10:35–37) it is only used to describe the attitude of Jesus and it reveals the divine nature of these acts within the context of the coming of the kingdom of God.[17] The Messianic use of the term as contained in the following verses: Mark 1:41, "Jesus was filled with compassion.[18] He reached out his hand and touched the man. "I am willing," he said. "Be clean!" Mark 6:33–34, "But many who saw them leaving recognized them and ran on foot from all the towns and got there ahead of them. When Jesus landed and saw a large crowd, he had compassion on them, because they were like sheep without a shepherd. So he began teaching them many things." Mark 8:2, "I have compassion for these people; they have already been with me three days and have nothing to eat." These texts characterize Jesus as "the Messiah in whom divine mercy is present" in concrete tangible ways (i.e., the feeding of the five thousand and the healing of the two blind men) instead of merely using the word to describe an emotional response to a dire situation.[19]

Further into the dynamic evolution and understanding of the word *compassion* we witness another distinct usage of this term in the writings of the Apostle Paul. Still maintaining the emotional quality of compassion, Paul uses the word only as a noun for the "whole man, the total personality at the deepest level"[20] that drives human behavior and interactions. In fact, his use of the term discloses the intimate quality of his relationship with recipients of his letters (Philemon v. 7 and 20, for example), but also as a way to characterize the nature of Christian engagement (Phil 2:1, "Therefore if you have any encouragement from being united with Christ, if any comfort from his love, if any common sharing in the Spirit, if any tenderness and compassion . . .").[21] Also, Paul uses the word "compassion" as "synonymous to love, which for him is the mutual experience and gift among

16. Elwell, ed., *Dictionary of Biblical Theology*, 109.
17. Ibid., 553.
18. A few manuscripts read "indignant" or "anger."
19. Elwell, ed., *Dictionary of Biblical Theology*, 554.
20. Ibid., 555.
21. Ibid.

Christians."[22] This is quite significant given the fact that compassion is not used frequently to speak of human relations in the pre-Christian period.[23] Paul re-dresses this traditional understanding, applies it to portray Christian dealings, which according to him is only made possible through one's relationship with Christ.[24]

We see a continuity of understanding compassion in this light in the rest of the New Testament where it is considered as one of the Christian virtues (Col. 3:12, "Therefore, as God's chosen people, holy and dearly loved, clothe yourselves with compassion, kindness, humility, gentleness and patience") believers of Christ must evidence.[25] The eschatological meaning (Luke 1:78, "because of the tender mercy of our God, by which the rising sun will come to us from heaven") attached to the word is also quite prominent in that "God's final act of revelation is seen as the outflowing of. . . God's heart-felt mercy . . . which leads the believer through perils of end time, will never abandon and gives abundantly to those who pray to God without ceasing."[26]

In sum, the biblical world offers a description of compassion that is both distinct from and yet complementary to other renderings of the word from other traditions. Seen from a biblical world view, compassion is inherent to God's essential nature whose first response is to show tender loving care to those who suffer and loving mercy in the face of betrayal and iniquities. As exemplified by Christ himself, this inner disposition fuels visible and concrete acts of kindness towards those who are vulnerable and in great need (e.g., the shepherding of the crowd, the feeding of the five thousand, and the healing of the blind). As recipients of God's compassion the people of God are then called to mirror and embody the same trait of loving care and mercy towards others, a truly remarkable expression of what it means to be a neighbor. In that light, the parable of the Good Samaritan serves as an icon of compassion in which the fullness of neighborly love fills the depth of the suffering and pain of another regardless of who this person might be.

However, the biblical understanding of compassion is not a "unique Christian response to suffering . . . even though Christians have unique

22. Ibid., 556.
23. Ibid., 553.
24. Ibid., 556.
25. Ibid.
26. Ibid., 558.

reasons for nurturing their compassionate dispositions."[27] Other wisdom traditions also consider compassion as an expression of altruistic love that is triggered when confronted with people suffering. In Buddhism, for example, compassion is described as "the wish that all beings be freed from suffering and the causes of suffering"[28] and that this intention is followed by "every method possible into action to remedy his torments."[29] The "causes of suffering" include not only the "immediate and visible causes . . . but also the deep-seated causes of suffering, chief of which is ignorance . . . the mistaken understanding of reality leading us to have disturbing mental states like hatred and compulsive desire."[30] Both the Christian and Buddhist tradition reveal a shared understanding of compassion as human response, both in intention and action, to suffering of others. They differ, however, in the source of suffering in that in Buddhism suffering is borne out of ignorance or misperception of reality whereas in Christianity the source lies much deeper than that. As explored earlier suffering emerges from the fallen state of the entire created order including human nature, which God has mercifully and compassionately dealt with through Christ. Here lies the unique reason for Christians to cultivate their compassionate dispositions. That is, it is a way of "paying it forward," as it were, of reciprocating to others the very gesture of unconditional love, tender mercy, and compassion shown to them by God in the first place. In some sense, compassion is a gift that keeps on giving that when it is unwrapped reveals the true heart of God enfleshed in human form and actualized in human action.

Compassion as a Distinct Emotion

At its rudimentary level, compassion is an emotional response that gets triggered in the sight of human suffering. From the perspective of psychology and neuroscience, it is a distinct emotion that when cultivated and practiced creates patterns of neural activation in the brain. This has been the subject of numerous discussions and scientific studies, which as we shall see later on complement and deepen our own theological conception of compassion. Gleaning from this emerging field of inquiry, in fact, opens up a new way of understanding and appreciating the pivotal role of

27. Elwell, ed., *Dictionary of Biblical Theology*, 109.
28. Ricard, *Altruism*, 26.
29. Ibid.
30. Ibid.

compassion in clarifying the nature (human identity), call (human solidarity), and destiny (human flourishing) of humanity.

Let us start by defining the word *emotion*. The literature on emotion research is in flux and varied depending on the context in which emotion is studied and defined. Generally, emotion is described as "episodic, relatively short term, biologically based patterns of perception, experience, physiology, action, and communication that occur in response to specific physical and social challenges and opportunities."[31] In other words, emotions arise as a result of a dynamic interplay between the person and the environment. Key in this exchange is the person's appraisal of what is going on and how much of it is perceived as relevant or valuable to the integrity of the experiencing self. The more personally relevant or consequential the appraised situation is the stronger the emotions will be. This subtle or sudden burst of emotional energy animates the person to act in a certain way either with intentionality or reactively in light of these appraisals.

Putting a lens on the subjective and emotional experience of Jesus upon seeing a multitude of people in Mark 6:33ff might help elucidate this point. Jesus' ministry is reaching its peak and his popularity is quickly spreading. This has aroused curiosity and interest among many. They started to follow and gather around Jesus whose image as a teacher, miracle worker, and leader of a small band of disciples is beginning to both impress and irritate people. Sensing their need to take a momentary respite and to get away from the crowd, he enjoined his disciples to "come away with him to a quiet place" (Mark 6:30–32). But the crowd's thirst to see and hear more of Jesus could not be quenched. Unmindful of Jesus and the disciples' need to rest their wearied bodies they "ran on foot from all the towns and got there ahead of them" (v. 33). When he reached their destination Jesus "saw a large crowd, he had compassion on them, because they were like sheep without a shepherd. So he began teaching them many things" (v. 34).

From the perspective of psychology of emotion, this singular description of Jesus' experience in that moment can be described in this manner. Jesus is placed in an environment with multiple stimuli vying for his attention—the presence and condition of his disciples, the place they went to, his own private thoughts and feelings, and the crowd. He is already interacting with these variables in varying degrees of intensity or levels of attention. Yet out of all these competing stimuli one stood out to him the most—he "saw the crowd." He could very well have continued on their journey and hid

31. Keltner and Gross, "Functional accounts of emotion," 468.

from the clamor and demands of these people. But he stopped in his tracks and looked deeply at those gathered around him. When he saw the crowd, he felt something quite distinct from feelings of empathy, sympathy, or pity.

Though these emotions share a common and benevolent orientation towards another, the difference between these emotions needs to be maintained. As previously stated, empathy is the ability to "put oneself in the shoes of another person," so to speak, to gain perspective, to get acquainted with the person's feelings and thoughts, and to understand the world as that person sees it.[32] Sympathy arises as a result of acknowledging the misfortune of another person and evokes feeling of concern or sorrow without necessarily entering into the internal world of that person. Whereas empathy inhabits the world of another to fully grasp his or her internal experience, sympathy remains on the outside looking in, recognizes the suffering of another, and then offers support. The last of this cluster of emotions is pity, which is often used interchangeably with compassion. However, the difference between these two affective states is stark in that pity sets up a rather uneven and hierarchical relationship with the person receiving the act of benevolent concern placed in an unequal or inferior position.

The story is very clear in stating what Jesus actually felt when he saw a throng of people waiting for him. He had compassion towards them because they were like sheep without a shepherd. The surge of emotional energy described as compassion came as a result of Jesus' appraisal or assessment of the situation—the crowd is like sheep scattered or harassed or in danger because they have no shepherd to feed and guide them. As the Good Shepherd (John 10:11) he felt compassion that was so strong it moved him literally to do something about what he saw. He began to teach them many things and later fed them with loaves of bread and fish.

The narrative contains three distinct yet related movements that comprise Jesus' experience of compassion. First, Jesus "saw" a large crowd— compassion as *bearing witness* to a particular situation. Second, Jesus "had" or felt compassion "because they were like sheep without a shepherd"— compassion as an *emotional response* arising out of a particular cognitive *appraisal* or assessment of the situation. Third, Jesus began to "teach" and later "fed" the crowd—compassion as an *engaged and active response* to help, alleviate, or fulfill a particular need. From a psychological perspective, we can describe compassion *as an emotional experience evoked by witnessing and appraising of another's situation or suffering, which subsequently leads to*

32. See Lazarus, *Emotion and Adaptation*.

intentional and concrete acts of service towards those who suffer and are vulnerable. Most assuredly, Jesus showed empathic concern towards the crowd by becoming aware of their condition. But he went beyond merely "feeling with them" and went out of his way to fulfill their physical (e.g., feeding of the five thousand) and spiritual hunger (e.g., teaching). Empathy fulfills the first two movements—bearing witness and emotional resonance—in a powerful way. In fact, it raises a red flag by drawing our attention "to the nature and intensity of the sufferings experienced by the other . . . . [I]t catalyzes the transformation of altruistic love into compassion."[33] Compassion encircles or completes these three movements—"sees and acknowledges," "resonates and appraises," and then "acts and intervenes"—in one fluid and engaged gesture of diffusive and fearless love.

Compassion as a Biological Imperative

Compassion as an emotion is a movement towards another—a person who is in need—and with it comes a desire or commitment to help, to suffer with, to alleviate suffering. The ubiquitous nature of suffering and the compassionate acts it elicits make us wonder if compassion is something innate or learned. This question has been the subject of reflection particularly by those keen on exploring the evolutionary basis of compassion. The Altruistic Brain Theory (ABT) discussed in the previous chapter is part of this burgeoning field and compassion research is a further refinement to that.

The science of compassion starts with the premise that "emotions are adaptations to particular survival and reproductive related situations"[34] or "inherited ancestral tools for living."[35] These emotional systems such as seeking, fear, rage, lust, care, panic, and play are organized in the brain and have helped our ancestors navigate a rather challenging, unpredictable, complicated environment.[36] Using animal models these basic emotional systems are located deep inside the brain (subcortical) and exist even before we can label, verbalize, or make sense of what we are feeling. This means that the "raw emotional tools for feeling and living are not created by lived experiences, although they may be shaped by them . . . . They are

33. Ricard, *Altruism,* 26.

34. Goetz et al., "Compassion," 354.

35. Fosha, Segel, and Solomon eds., *The Healing Power of Emotion,* 4.

36. Ibid., 3.

ancestral memories, successful solutions to living encoded in genetically dictated brain systems."[37]

One of the seven basic or primary emotional systems is the care/nurturance system. The survival of infants is solely dependent on the caretaking behaviors of the mother, which has already been primed prior to birth.[38] Several hormonal and neuronal changes occur before the arrival of the infant that help the mother attune to the needs of her newborn. This includes "increasing estrogen, prolactin and oxytocin . . . sensitizing her brain to help assure that interaction with the newborn is a special delight."[39] Particularly, the production of oxytocin during breastfeeding and sensitive and sustained touching by the mother to her infant "facilitate strong bonding with offspring—brain changes that are foundational for nurturant love."[40]

This nourishing experience is further characterized by an outpouring of compassion especially when the infant is in distress.

The precarious condition of the offspring and the instinctual response of the mother to reach out and caretake forms the basis for the biology of compassion. The "vulnerable offspring argument"[41] considers compassion as a distinct emotional response or caregiving system aimed at providing physical safety and psychological nurturance towards those vulnerable offspring. This intuitive or instinctual capacity for attunement acts as a shield to protect the young from harm and suffering, therefore assuring the offspring's "survival and reproductive viability"[42] in the future. Over time this becomes ingrained and diffusive to include attunement to suffering of those outside familial bonds.

Another evolutionary approach to compassion is set within the context of "sexual selection theory."[43] The choice of a mate is dependent on the person's ability to feel with and to act kindly towards another, which then foreshadows the "compassionate reproductive partner to devote more resources to offspring, to provide physical care—protection, affection, and touch—and to create cooperative, caring communities so vital to the

37. Ibid., 5–6.
38. Ibid., 13.
39. Ibid.
40. Ibid.
41. Ibid.
42. Ibid.
43. Ibid.

survival of the offspring."[44] In fact, it has been demonstrated that those who grew up in this type of an enriched environment not only survive but thrive and live meaningful and connected lives.[45] The flow of compassion from attuned parents to vulnerable offspring and between intimate partners act as a catalyst for subsequent feelings of affinity and human solidarity with non-kin. Within this relational exchange, "compassion emerged as a state to motivate altruism in mutually beneficial relationships and contexts."[46]

All this is to show that compassion is deeply embedded in human nature and by extension is sculpted and supported by our physical body and brain. Let us dig deeper into how our body and brain respond or change when we practice compassion. The autonomic nervous system, which is part of the peripheral nervous system, serves a "regulatory function" that ensures the body adapts optimally to various internal and environment demands.[47] This includes an activation of "emotion-related tendencies, from fight to flight tendencies to withdrawal, or in the case of compassion, approach and caregiving."[48] Studies have shown that acts of compassion, that is, focused orientation towards someone in need, is correlated with the heart rate going down from baseline levels.[49] In turn, the inhibition of heart rate promotes approach, soothing, and pro-social behavior, which supports the action tendency to alleviate the suffering of another. Indeed, a calm and relaxed state of being is a necessary condition to effect change especially during times of distress and difficulties.

A primary component of autonomic nervous system that is also associated with pro-social behavior like compassion is the vagus nerve, which is a bundle of neural pathways exiting from areas of the brainstem that are responsible for regulating several organs, including the heart.[50] The capacity for adaptive flexibility (e.g., the fight-or-flight response in the face of life-threatening situations as well as pursuing pro-social behavior in safe environments) is a result of a "myelinated vagus nerve . . . in which inhibition and recovery of the vagal tone to the heart can rapidly mobilize or calm

44. Ibid.

45. see Bowlby, *Attachment and Loss,* and subsequent literature on attachment theory.

46. Ibid., 355.

47. Harmon-Jones and Beer, eds., *Methods in Social Neuroscience,* 119.

48. Goetz et al., "Compassion," 362.

49. Ibid.

50. Porges, *The Polyvagal Theory,* 27.

an individual."[51] In other words, our physical body is intricately designed to respond to various life situations often rapidly and outside of conscious awareness. We run or hide when confronted with a threatening event or approach and pursue social connections when feeling safe and secure.

According to the polyvagal theory our "emotional states are dependent upon the lower brain regulation of the visceral state" which in turn "foster different domains of behavior."[52] One of these domains that is intertwined or connected to the "muscles of the face and head and the myelinated vagal fiber"[53] is the social engagement system. In fact, evidence shows that there is a distinct facial expression connected to compassion, which is characterized by "oblique eyebrows and concerned gaze"[54] signaling a desire to reach out and help. Internally, this system is also capable of downregulating the sympathetic nervous system—which readies the body for a fight-or-flight response when under threat—and calms the viscera or guts and regulates facial muscles.[55] This carefully orchestrated physiological response enables and supports positive social interactions, which includes acting compassionately towards those in need.

Compassion and the Brain

As previously discussed, compassion is a combination of distinct emotional states, inferences, and appraisals we make about the other's suffering, and the attendant behavior or action to help relieve it. These components are sculpted or supported by specific neural circuitry or patterns in the brain. Recently, there is an emerging body of research that looks specifically into the neural correlates or underpinnings of compassion.[56] Contiguously, studies have also shown that those engaged in compassion cultivation training and practices are reaping the benefits of strong immune system and adaptive behavioral responses to combat stress,[57] reduction of post-traumatic stress disorder symptoms,[58] improved health and general well-

51. Ibid., 121.
52. Fosha, Segel, and Solomon, eds., *The Healing Power of Emotion*, 52.
53. Ibid., 41.
54. Keltner, "The Compassionate Instinct."
55. Fosha, Segel, and Solomon eds., *The Healing Power of Emotion*, 41.
56. Immordino-Yang et al., "Neural correlates of admiration and compassion."
57. Pace, "Effect of compassion meditation."
58. Sepalla, "Breathing-based meditation."

being,[59] and enhanced compassion, resilience, and patient care among healthcare providers.[60]

There are at least several neural networks that are implicated or associated with compassion.[61] The first network involves the dorsal medial prefrontal cortex (dmPFC), temporoparietal junction (TPJ), and posterior cingulate cortex (PCC), which supports the ability to empathize or infer, intuit, or appraise the condition or situation of another person.[62] The second network recruits the ventral mid-anterior insular cortex (aI), dorsal anterior cingulate (dACC), and their connections with the amygdala, which supports emotional responses to the suffering of others.[63] These two brain systems are linked with the cognitive (appraisal mode) and affective (emotional mode) components of compassion. But as we know, compassion is also about having the motivation or desire to act or behave in a manner that alleviates the suffering of the other. It other words, it is action oriented. There is a strong pull to step in and take action to remedy the situation and provide concrete acts of loving-kindness and compassion to the person in pain and suffering. This equally important aspect of compassion is also reflected in the brain via the ventromedial prefrontal cortex (vmPFC), which translates conceptual information into affective behavioral and physiological responses, among others.[64] Of course, the vmPFC is not a stand-alone brain part that is correlated with the action tendencies of compassion. It is connected to the neural networks identified above as well as to the striatum, hypothalamus, and brain stem, which when activated perform comprehensive system-wide cognitive, affective, physiological, and behavioral responses.[65]

Using this level of analysis to describe Jesus' experience in the aforementioned passage yields the following interpretation. The compassion he feels upon seeing the crowd is an emotional experience laden with meaning—the crowd is like sheep without a shepherd (cognitive and affective neural networks activated)—and action: the teaching and feeding (physiological and behavioral networks activated). The emotional meaning Jesus

59. Sepalla, "Social connection and compassion."
60. Sepalla, "Loving-kindness meditation."
61. Shamay-Tsoory, "Two systems for empathy."
62. Frith et al., "The neural basis of mentalizing."
63. Duerden et al., "Lateralization of affective processing in the insula."
64. Haber et al., "The reward circuit."
65. Roy, "Ventromedial prefrontal sub-cortical systems."

attached to what he saw reveals how deeply he feels towards those eagerly waiting for him, indicating two psychological processes that are intricately involved in the subjective experience of compassion, namely, 1) the valuing of the other,[66] and 2) evaluating the other in relation to the self.[67] Jesus' deep abiding love towards people reveals their value and worth as well as their connection and relevance to his mission and ministry. Neuroimaging studies have shown the activation of vmPFC-subcortical circuitry when tracking emotional connection with others[68] and pro-social behaviors towards those needing help.[69] A dynamic-process model of compassion has been proposed to clarify the intricate relationship of these processes.[70] Going back to the narrative discussed earlier, this particular brain-based model of compassion can be described as follows. After seeing the throng of people, a feeling of compassion arises in Jesus, primarily because of the inference or appraisal he made about the condition of the crowd—they are like sheep without a shepherd. This is represented as "unique patterns of neural activity within the insular-cingulate network and the dmPFC, TPJ, and PCC. These patterns of activity are integrated in the medial pre-frontal-striatal network, along with additional information, to form an emotional meaning."[71] The emotional meaning is constructed out of the personal significance of the crowd to Jesus—as the Good Shepherd of the sheep. These neural networks conspire or mutually influence each other such that there is a "formation of a stable, coherent, system-wide representation of the feelings, thoughts, and narrative surrounding the encounter, leading to a coordinated behaviors including helping."[72] In this case, such an emotionally charged encounter moved Jesus to show compassion through teaching and feeding of the five thousand. These external acts of compassion are reflected intricately as patterns of circuitry in the brain.

66. Batson, *Altruism in Humans*.

67. Goetz et al., "Compassion."

68. Krienen et al., "Clan mentality."

69. Zaki et al., "Equitable decision making."

70. Ashar, "Towards a neuroscience of compassion."

71. Ibid.

72. Ibid.

The Face of Compassion

So far, we have traversed various territories or disciplines—from Bible-theology to psychology to neuroscience—and have gleaned from each of them essential truths that when integrated might provide a richer, more nuanced, and layered description of compassion. Let us then weave these ideas together and create what we call a mosaic of compassion.

We are wired for compassion. It is part of human nature. It is in our DNA. This innate capacity that is triggered when confronted with suffering is layered with specific emotional states, thought processes, and behaviors seamlessly working in concert together to alleviate the suffering of another. Wishing for and working towards the betterment of the other is the ultimate goal of this benevolent act. It sets aside all self-preoccupations in favor of an unbridled enthusiasm in championing the cause and welfare of the other. This pro-social and affiliative response generated by compassion is supported and mediated by specific circuitry or patterns in the brain that can be harnessed or cultivated so that it becomes a human trait, a way of engaging the world that is awash with so much pain and suffering.

For followers of Christ, the practice and cultivation of compassion takes on a new significance. At its core, compassion is a way of mirroring the heart of God whose solidarity and intimate regard for the welfare of humanity is expressed in Jesus Christ, the compelling portrait of compassionate presence. Given the universal nature of suffering and in particular to mitigate the problem of otherization done in the name of religion, reclaiming the centrality of compassion as the pulsating heartbeat of the Christian life becomes all the more pressing and paramount. After all, being compassionate is inherent in who we are as created in the image of a compassionate, loving, and merciful God.

The root of compassion runs deep. It emerges from a soil that is nourished by a profound awareness of the connection and interdependence of all sentient beings. It bursts forth and makes room for the other. It spreads inward and produces a sense of well-being and personal satisfaction. Given the enormous reach and depth of compassion in alleviating and transforming suffering it behooves us to think of practices that might help nourish and grow this innate human disposition in us. The next chapter tackles this very issue by exploring the role of training the mind and heart to bear the fruit of compassion.

Chapter Four

Compassionate Mind

In a world that is fraught with suffering and pain, compassion offers rest, help, and healing. In a world that is ravaged by division and alienation compassion bridges the divide and makes us acutely aware of our common humanity. In a world that questions the integrity of the Christian church, compassion becomes a beacon of light that authenticates the Christian message of radical love. Compassionate love defines who we are as followers of Christ and through it the world knows that we are his disciples (John 13:35).

Like many virtues, however, compassion needs to be cultivated if it is to grow and become second nature to us. A way to accomplish this is through the transformation of our mind (Rom 12:2), a process integral to the Christian life. In concert with the Holy Spirit (Rom 8:9–11; Col 3:10) this process of renewal deepens our capacity to discern the will and working of God over and against the prevalent zeitgeist.[1] In other words, we begin to imbue the "mind of Christ" that reflects in thoughts, words, and character God's compassionate heart towards a broken and suffering world.

However, before exploring what the "mind of Christ" means and what "renewal of the mind" looks like it might be helpful to clarify at the outset Scripture's definition of the word "mind." Both in the Old and New Testament the word "mind" or *nous* connotes a variety of things. In the Old Testament, the term *mind* encompasses a broad range of ideas meant to "describe the inward or invisible dimensions of the human beings in a holistic manner."[2] Depending on the context and the purpose of the word, this may include the "seat of a person's thought and emotional life, the emo-

1. Elwell, ed., *Dictionary of Biblical Theology*, 527.
2. Ibid.

tions, and more broadly, to the inner person."[3] This more holistic use of the word in the Old Testament reflects the Hebrew culture that emphasizes the whole person in all of its dimensions. Thus, heart, soul, and mind are not separate entities but "each is a reference to the whole inner person and is to be viewed in relation to the body."[4] For example, in such verses as 2 Chronicles 12:14; Deuteronomy 31:1; Isaiah 46:8; 1 Kings 3:12; Proverbs 18:15; Proverbs 16:1; and Genesis 20:5 we see the word *heart* used in various senses to include the person's way of "thinking, perceiving, and willing to being," bringing together the ideas of knowledge, understanding, and will.[5]

Another Hebrew term, *ruah*, which means "spirit," is also used to describe the inner person from the "perspective of the mind, understanding, and reason."[6] It can also refer to various mental capacities—"from skills to planning" and "conscious thoughts" or "mind-set" (Exod 28:3; 1 Chr 28:12; Ezek 11:5; Dan 5:20).[7] A related word *nepes* or soul is also used to characterize the inner person in terms of the "intellectual or mental dimension of life,"[8] as in Deuteronomy 6:5 where the "soul, along with the heart" takes the "whole inner person as a thinking, knowing, and willing force, which must decide to serve God."[9]

In the New Testament, we find the word *nous* commonly used in the writings of the Apostle Paul.[10] The definition of this word ranges from one's "worldview, disposition and inner orientation or moral inclination (for example see Rom 1:28; Eph 4:17; Col 2:18), or an organ that determines the course of action (Rom 7:23), or the state (or act) of understanding (Luke 24:25; 1 Cor 14:14–15, 19; Phil 4:7)."[11]

Paul employs this word to make a distinction between a way of thinking or understanding that either promotes *or* contradicts the will of God.[12]

3. Ibid., 528.
4. Ibid.
5. Ibid.
6. Ibid.
7. Ibid.
8. Ibid.
9. Ibid.
10. Ibid.
11. Ibid.
12. Ibid., 529.

In this cursory discussion we discover that both the Old Testament and New Testament define the word "mind" generally as 1) the whole person in all its dimensions and totality, and specifically as 2) a thought system or the faculty of conscious reflection and perception. The mind is where decisions are made and it is with the mind that one chooses (volition) to reflect or reject God. The New Testament adds another layer to our understanding of the mind by relating its condition to conversion. Renewal is the result of the Holy Spirit working in us, which makes apprehension of divine matters possible. Before this, the mind is described as futile and blind. While it is true that renewal is necessary, still the decision to employ the mind to apprehend God remains our responsibility.[13]

The process of renewal entails the transformation of the whole person with the mind conceived as mental faculty its entry point. During this process the mind is being buoyed to have the "mind of Christ," that is, to follow his example of *kenosis* or self-emptying (Phil 2), which is the hallmark of compassion. Compassion involves the willingness to empty ourselves of our ego-centered preoccupations and obsessions so that we can give full and loving attention to those who suffer and to offer them a hospitable space where they can feel safe, respected, honored, helped, and accompanied. When this space is created, sustained acts of compassion mark a journey one takes *with* another and not done *for* or *to* the other. We endeavor to explore this core foundation—compassion as *kenosis*—more fully now given its significance in inspiring and sustaining this expression of altruistic love.

A life lived in unity is a theme that Paul frequently addresses in most of his epistles. In the first two chapters of Philippians alone, we see Paul's admonition to have "one mind" repeated twice within the span of six verses (Phil 1:27 and Phil 2:2). This appeal for unity springs from the knowledge that the Philippian church is united in Christ, comforted by his love, enjoined by the Spirit, and embraced by the tenderness and compassion of Christ himself (Phil 2:1). There is no other motivation towards the pursuit of unity other than a life that is in and shared with Christ. Being recipients of God's benevolence through Christ, the church is enjoined to extend these same blessings to others (Phil 2:5–11) without conditions or reservations and in a manner that expresses oneness in mind, love, spirit, and purpose (Phil 2:2).

13. Ibid., 530.

Concretely, the call for unity is tied to one's disavowal and removal of the self on the throne and in humility putting others there. This act of self-denial and movement towards esteeming others better than oneself and caring for them and their interests as we do our own (Phil 2:3) flows out of the diffusiveness and sufficiency of Christ's love and keen interest towards us. The Christ-in-me–self-regard that compels us towards other-regard marks our "true identity . . . [,] the common journey of giving ourselves away for the sake of the others."[14]

Of particular importance to this discussion is the emphasis placed by Paul on admonishing the church to be of the "same mind," which is repeated twice in this passage. The Greek verb *phroneo* is not restricted to only mean a world view or outlook that influences perception and behaviors.[15] In this particular context, Paul is encouraging his readers to take on the mind of Christ, a mind that is synchronous with the will of God[16] and bears fruit of humility as exemplified by Christ himself in Philippians 2:5–8.

Imitating Christ

After this short but direct call to be other-focused Paul draws our attention back to Christ as he summons his readers to have the mind-set of Christ Jesus as they relate to one another (Phil 2:5). This is not just about instructing the church "what they should believe about Christ. It is rather to show how they should act in light of the pattern of Jesus' cruciform love"[17] through mutual self-giving and sacrifice.

Though the call to have the mind of Christ is for everyone, it is deeply personal and therefore must be intentionally internalized and cultivated. After all, the life we project onto the world is an expression of and intimately linked to our interior life. We catch a glimpse of this power of congruence between the inner and outer life through Christ who "was in the form of God, inwardly possessing the divine nature, outwardly displaying the divine glory."[18] Hence, any act of compassion must flow and flourish

14. Flemming, *Philippians*, 105.
15. Elwell, ed., *Dictionary of Biblical Theology*, 528.
16. Ibid., 529.
17. Flemming, *Philippians*, 112.
18. Motyer, *The Message of Philippians*, 74.

naturally from the garden of our heart awakened and sustained by habituating the mind of Christ every day all day.

Considered as the Hymn of Christ[19] by many, Philippians 2:6–8 el-
evates Christ's attitude or mind-set of self-emptying as the epitome, the
standard, and the true embodiment of humility. Christ's intentional descent
to become "nothing, taking the form or nature of a servant, being made in
human likeness" (v. 6) is for us a shining paradigmatic example of what it
means to relate to each other. Of course, he did not have to do this. But
he did. He chose to surrender his divine privileges so that we can share
in his divine glory. The grave importance (i.e., patterning our lives after
the example of Christ) and consequence (i.e., the salvation of humanity) of
Christ's self-emptying is rooted in the fact that he, "who, being in the nature
of God, did not consider equality with God something to be grasped" (v. 6).
But what exactly does this verse mean? And how might the understanding
of self-emptying help illumine the kind of attitude, mind-set, or lifestyle we
need to embody as people of compassion? To answer these questions, we
will take a brief excursion into how biblical scholars have interpreted this
verse.

The word "form" or *morphe* in Greek has been translated in various
ways—including God's "essential nature," "image," "mode of being," and
"status."[20] Contextually, the phrase *"in the form of God"* refers to "either the
visible manifestation of God, or one that holds the actual essence or nature
of God."[21] Either of these translations works, given what the passage is suggesting theologically about who Christ is. That is, Christ is the "image of the
invisible God" (Col 1:15) preexistent and has demonstrated the "majesty
and splendor or the divine glory,"[22] and is the "very essence of God."[23]

Yet, despite of all that, "he did not consider his equality with God as
something to be used for his advantage" (Phil 2:6). He did not revel, get
comfortable, or hold onto his nature or essence tightly or get fixated on
his eternal glory and status that due his name. Instead, he gave up *all* that,
dispossessed it, and made himself nothing so that we can gain everything
that is available to us as sons and daughters of God. In the words of another
author,

19. Martin, *A Hymn of Christ*, 37.

20. Fabricatore, *Form of God, Form of Servant*, 143–152.

21. Ibid., 154.

22. Flemming, *Philippians*, 113.

23. Ibid., 156.

Christ Jesus before the incarnation, was equal to God and displayed the splendor of God's glory. When he came into the world, however, he did not take advantage of these privileges. He subjected himself to humiliation for the sake of human being (cf. 2 Cor. 8:9). The contrast of Jesus with Adam is striking since Adam in the garden strove to be equal to God and thus rejected God's lordship in eating the fruit of the tree. Christ, on the contrary, though possessing equality with God (in this respect he differs from Adam), did not use his status as a means of enriching himself. Indeed, precisely because he was in the form of God and was equal with God, he refused to use his position as a means of self-aggrandizement. He used his status as a platform for giving and self-surrender, not as a bridgehead for praise and self-exaltation. The cross, not the crown, was his path to glory.[24]

This incarnation motif—of Christ taking on human flesh for our sake—is spelled out in the following verse: ". . . by taking the very nature of a servant, being made in human likeness" (v.7) to once again put a spotlight on Christ's overflowing generosity and deep compassion for humanity. He poured his life out for us so that we can have the fullness of life (John 10:10), he became poor so that we can become rich (2 Cor 8:9), and took the form of a slave so that we can be freed from the bondage of sin and death (Rom 8:2).

The plight of slaves in the Greco-Roman context is one where they were bereft of basic human rights, without status, and owned as a property by their masters.[25] In other words, they were nobodies, and their humanity forgotten or obscured. Yes, Christ willingly took the "appearance and characteristics of a slave . . . spurning the right to rank and reputation in the eyes of people, he identified with the lowest of the low and the poorest of the poor."[26] This is a tall order for us who are called to have the mind of Christ in our dealings with each other. How challenging it is to do this when one is bombarded by an unremitting call to place one's own interest above all others.

But the extent of Christ's example of humility does not end with him taking the qualities of a slave and becoming flesh that walked on this earth. He went further, according to verse 8: "And being found in appearance as a man, he humbled himself by becoming obedient to death—even death

---

24. Thomas Schreiner, cited in Fabricatore, *Form of God, Form of Servant*, 143–52.

25. Flemming, *Philippians*, 116.

26. Ibid.

on a cross!" Yes, he subjected himself to experience the extreme form of humiliation—death on the cross. During the Roman times, "crucifixion was the ultimate instrument of Roman torture, used as a political tool to subjugate the provinces of the empire. It was reserved for those with no status, like despised slaves, hardened criminals and rebellious peasants."[27] And yet despite of all the jeers, shame, and utter humiliation heaped on him as he was paraded through the street he bore that cross in silent obedience. He surrendered his own will to the purposes of the Father by subjecting himself to utter humiliation by dying on the cross, the "final downward step of self-abasement."[28] The impact and consequence of such sacrificial act is cosmic (John 1:29; Rom 3:25–26; Gal 3:13–14; Col 2:13–14) and its implication for how one should conduct one's life in relation to others is specific. Paul offers the Philippian church the example of humility demonstrated by Christ himself as the paradigm for human relationships. Like Christ whose single-mindedness and firm conviction to obey the Father is absolute, they, too, must be willing "to take the downward path of dishonour, suffering, and self-renouncing love."[29]

In the last three verses of the passage we are considering we see Christ lifted up from the lowest of the low to the highest place imaginable— "Therefore God exalted him to the highest place and gave him the name that is above every name, that at the name of Jesus every knee should bow, in heaven and on earth and under the earth, and every tongue acknowledge that Jesus Christ is Lord to the glory of God the Father" (Phil 2:9–11). Christ's self-renunciation and humility is met with God's exaltation of him and conferring on him the name Jesus as Lord of All worthy of praise, honour, and glory. Christ is exalted "because he emptied himself and in obedience embraced the cross"[30] and in that lowly sordid state we encounter God with us. Christ who "stands in solidarity with the poor and powerless, the suffering and vulnerable, the lowly and the marginalized"[31] now sits on the throne to be worshipped as Lord of the universe.

As said previously, having the mind of Christ means being shaped by Christ's own example of self-emptying, the true mark of compassion. We serve the other not out of a sense of duty but out of deep commitment to

27. Flemming, *Philippians*, 141.
28. Marcus Bockmuehl, cited in ibid., 142.
29. Ibid., 119.
30. Ibid., 123.
31. Ibid.

God who calls us to pursue unity and love. We serve the other not to merit their approval, acceptance, and esteem. We serve in self-emptying love as a way of honoring Christ by infusing his story into ours, by living under his lordship not ours, thereby bringing glory to the Father. The focus remains outward to others and upward to God, and the motive power of compassion lies in the fact that we are "united in Christ" (Phil 2:1).

Transforming the Mind

How then do we imbue the mind of Christ in us? Patterning one's life after Christ occurs through the renewal of the mind (Rom 12:2), which is a process that can be "sustained by the conscious decision to maintain communication and commitment to God."[32] The first two verses of Romans 12 are considered to be the practical and ethical application of the preceding eleven chapters, which are primarily theological or doctrinal in emphasis.[33] Paul summons his readers to a life of righteousness as a fitting response to receiving "God's abundant provision of grace and of the gift of righteousness reign in life through the one man, Jesus Christ" (Rom 5:17; see also Rom 3:25). For him, there is a fluid connection between receiving the transformation internally initiated by God in Christ and a life of transformation that springs forth externally to others. So, what are these lifestyle changes Paul is asking churches in Rome to manifest?

First is to "offer your bodies as a living sacrifice, holy and pleasing to God—this is your true and proper worship" (Rom. 12:1). According to Paul, God's lavish but costly gift and act of mercy must be met with a whole-hearted and complete self-emptying or surrender of oneself—body, mind, and spirit—to God. Since the work of God in us permeates every aspect of our being, in the same way, we are to offer our total personhood, "every area of life, and [this] includes the body in all of its particularity and concreteness"[34] back to God who gives and requires all. The cultic language[35]—"offer," "sacrifice," and "worship"—employed by Paul in verse one is worth noting. The powerful imagery contained in this language is connected to the various sacrifices made in temples and shrines still operative

---

32. Elwell, ed., *Dictionary of Biblical Theology*, 529.
33. Hultgren, *Paul's Letter to the Romans*, 435.
34. Schreiner, *Romans*, 644.
35. Hultgren, *Paul's Letter to the Romans*, 439.

at that time.[36] The only but major difference here is the fact that Christians are to offer themselves as a "living sacrifice" in contrast to the "offering of animals that have been slain or no longer living."[37] This implies a large degree of intentionality, willingness, or choice that must be carried out on a regular and daily manner from the one doing the sacrifice, as a response to God's own willful intention to make us righteous through the final and complete sacrificial act of Christ.

Our bodies or entire beings must not only be offered as a living sacrifice, they must also be "holy" or set apart and "pleasing to God." Yes! There is only one reason for this act of loving surrender and unreserved consecration, and that is to please God and God alone. This wholehearted response to God's mercy, according to Paul, is our "true and proper worship," and is not confined to merely "somatic, bodily compliance—'going through the motions'—or pneumatic, irrational emotionalism—'worship experiences'—or to worship in the sense of religious activities confined in the sanctuary."[38] A true spiritual worship, in response to God's action and transformation within, entails the whole person living out in the world a transformed life in "sacrificial service or obedience"[39] to God. This includes "personal and social ethics as much as corporate and private spiritual disciplines."[40]

Essential to the Christian life is the daily renewing of the mind (Rom 12:2a) that acts as a shield or buffer from the influences of a depraved and deceptive age. Here, Paul is making a distinction between the present age, which is in direct opposition to God and the new age that has been inaugurated by Christ. This new and present age refers to the "present world in which people exist, having its own ethos and standards, and which can be characterized as evil, under the dominion of its own divinity, and doomed to pass away."[41] In other words, it is a world that stands contrary to the purposes of God. Instead of "conforming to this age" Paul makes a strong appeal for believers to be "transformed by the renewal of the mind." As pointed earlier, the term "mind" refers to various things—from a thought system of beliefs and ways of seeing and understanding the world to that

36. Ibid., 540.
37. Ibid.
38. Greathouse, *Romans 9–16*, 130.
39. Hultgren, *Paul's Letter to the Romans*, 141.
40. Greathouse, *Romans 9–16*, 131.
41. Hultgren, *Paul's Letter to the Romans*, 441.

human faculty or organ where conscious reflection and perception occurs to the whole person itself.[42] Since patterns of thinking shape human behavior, Paul strongly exhorts believers to ensure that their thoughts, mind-set, and ways of apprehending the world are subjected to the transformative action of the Holy Spirit. Of course, the transformation that occurs is not limited only to having right thoughts or a right way of thinking. The transformation that occurs in the level of cognition slips into other aspects of the person in its totality such that mind of Christ and Christlike life becomes more evident and palpable for people witnessing this metamorphosis.

The overall intent and outcome for this call to renewal should not be missed. According to Paul, it is only through this ongoing, dynamic, and intentional process of subjecting our mind to the transformation of the Holy Spirit that we can "test and approve what God's will is—his good, pleasing and perfect will" (Rom 2:2b). This world, this present age is replete with philosophies and world views, secular or Christian, that directly or subtly contradict the gospel of Christ. Hence, discernment or the process of testing, discovering, and approving[43] is key in distinguishing God's will from the wiles of this world. The daily renewal of the mind is the scaffolding that supports and sustains the process of discerning the will of God for our lives. And when this good, pleasing, and perfect will is carried out in the concreteness of our daily living it becomes a fragrant offering in which God takes delight.

Though Paul did not offer explicit directives on this process of renewing the mind, it is important to note that the "means of transformation does not bypass human personality or the brain."[44] In fact the ability to apprehend divine matters and the response one makes in light of this understanding occurs through the "operation of the mind,"[45] or the organ itself, the brain.

The Brain in Mind

It is quite evident that the Bible has a unique understanding of the word *mind*, which has to be maintained to appreciate the message Paul is trying

---

42. Elwell, ed., *Dictionary of Biblical Theology*, 530.

43. Hultgren, *Paul's Letter to the Romans*, 442.

44. Schreiner, *Romans*, 648.

45. Ibid.

to convey. Keeping this definition in view, we will set out on a different path, a journey in search for another way of defining the words *mind* and *brain* from other domains of knowledge. This search is guided by the following questions: 1) How have other disciplines defined mind and brain? 2) How might their conceptions of these words help expand our understanding of Paul's call for the renewal of mind?

The brain is the three-pound corrugated gray matter encased within and protected by the skull. Considered the most complex organ in the body, it contains billions of neurons that are constantly sending electrical signals to each other as a way to "help maintain the whole body in an optimal state relative to the environment, in order to maximize the chances of survival. The brain does this by registering stimuli and then responding by generating actions. In the process, it also generates subjective experience such as thoughts or emotions."[46] This beautifully complex, coordinated, and complicated process evolved through many stages over a significant period of time in response to environmental challenges. In the human brain these challenges mostly take shape in the form of "complex social systems,"[47] where family and group relationships are formed, tested, stretched, and forged to ensure survival and reproductive success.

When it comes to relating the brain with the mind it is important to think of them as "two aspects of one complex system . . . . [I]n complementary fashion, mental activity and behavior depend on the physically determinate operations of the brain, itself a physicochemical system."[48] Changes that occur in the physical structures of the brain will result in changes in mental activities and vice versa, again underscoring this "unitary complex system."[49] The importance of conscious mental life, which is central to the book's premise, "exerts potent causal effects on the interplay of cerebral operations . . . . In the position of top command at the highest levels in the hierarchy of brain organization, the subjective properties were seen to exert control over the biophysical and chemical activities at subordinate levels."[50]

The causal power of the mind in shaping or changing the structure of the brain begs for a focused discussion of the mind's properties and functions. Various disciplines have offered a definition of the mind that is very

46. Carter, *The Human Brain Book*, 38.
47. Dunbar, "The social brain."
48. Jeeves, *Minds, Brains, Souls and Gods*, 34.
49. Ibid., 35.
50. Gregory, ed., *The Oxford Companion to the Mind*, 164–65.

particular and therefore restrictive to their unique context.[51] In an attempt to provide a working definition that has greater applicability to various domains of inquiry the following has been proposed.

1. A core aspect of the human mind is an embodied and relational process that regulates the flow of energy and information within the brain and between brains.

2. The mind as an emergent property of the body and relationships is created within internal neurophysiological processes and relational experiences. In other words, the mind is a process that emerges from the distributed nervous system extending throughout the entire body, and also from the communication patterns that occur within relationships.

3. The structure and function of the developing brain are determined by how the experience, especially within interpersonal relationships, shapes the genetically programmed maturation of the nervous systems.[52]

The definition proffered highlights the biological (physical substrate) as well as the relational components (social substrate) of the mind and how each contributes to the mind's constitution and expression. Relationships, whether by synaptic connections in the brain or between individuals or groups interacting with each other, are a key defining feature of the inner workings of the mind. Conceived in this manner, this creates an opportunity to become more intentional in discerning how best to nurture relationships that facilitate brain health and human flourishing.

Current research on brain science is also yielding fruits of immense and practical significance. It has been widely accepted that the human brain reaches a certain stage in adulthood where it becomes fixed or relatively stable. This, of course, no longer holds. Various experimental studies reveal that the "living brain constantly changing its functional and structural properties depending on changing inputs and experiences."[53] A well-publicized study indicates that London taxi drivers have a larger hippocampus compared to a control group.[54] The hippocampus is located

51. Siegel, *The Developing Mind*, 28.
52. Ibid., 30.
53. Villringer et al., "Plasticity of the human brain," 2.
54. Maguire et al., "Navigation-related structural change."

in the limbic system and is associated with memory and spatial navigation, which are critical mental faculties necessary to navigate the busy and weblike streets of London. The brain's ability to reorganize its structure and function induced by novel and sustained experiences is called neuroplasticity.

One of the ways to induce neuroplasticity is meditation because it sharpens the capacity for focused attention. As we know, attention is more than just a mental faculty alongside other cognitive functions such as perception, language, and memory. In fact, it is considered to have an "ontological status . . . of something prior to functions and even to things. Attention changes what kind of a thing comes into being for us: in that way it changes the world . . . . Attention also changes who we are, we who are doing the attending."[55] Simply put, our way of being in the world and its attendant beliefs, orientation, thoughts, and feelings is profoundly shaped by this innate human capacity, by what we choose to attend to, which in turn shapes who we are.

So whatever the focus of our attention might be, our brain responds by strengthening or growing neural connections. Meditation is one such activity that facilitates neuroplasticity. Broadly defined, meditation is a "family of complex emotional and attentional regulatory strategies developed for various ends, including the cultivation of well-being and emotional balance."[56] To prove this point a study has been conducted to compare the brain activity of novice meditators with Buddhist monks whose lives are characterized by countless hours of meditation. Participants were asked to practice compassion meditation, which engendered feelings of loving-kindness to all sentient beings. Brain scans revealed a dramatic increase in brain activity during compassion meditation among Buddhist monks compared to their counterparts.

> Activity in the left prefrontal cortex (the seat of positive emotions such happiness) swamped activity in the right prefrontal (site of negative emotions and anxiety), something never before seen from purely mental activity. A sprawling circuit that switches on at the sight of suffering also showed greater activity in the monks. So did regions responsible for planned movement, as if the monks' brains were itching to go to the aid of those in distress.[57]

55. McGilchrist, *The Master and his Emissary*, 28.
56. Davidson et al., "Neuroplasticity and Meditation," 176.
57. Begley, "Scans of monks' brains," B1.

The outcome of this study is quite exciting. It shows that compassion meditation leads to the activation of mirror neuron system in the brain, which is the social circuitry responsible for interpersonal attunement via increased levels of empathy and compassion towards others.[58] The unifying effects of this meditative practice promote a sense of personal well-being, which spills over to pro-social and affiliative behaviors and ethical values.[59]

The implications of a dynamic, experience-dependent, and plastic brain are far reaching on many levels. When this knowledge is paired with the Apostle Paul's call for the renewal of the mind we come to realize just how important spiritual disciplines or habits of the soul (e.g., meditation) are in transforming our entire being—body, mind, and spirit—to reflect the character of God. More specifically, this landmark discovery casts light on the myriad ways we can transform our mind and rewire our brain to support and enhance our commitment to embody compassionate love to all.

The writers of the Scriptures were acutely aware of the immense power of meditation in focusing one's attention towards God. We see various admonitions to meditate the law of the Lord day and night (Josh 1:8; Ps 1:2), to meditate on God's unfailing love (Ps 48:9), on his works and mighty deeds (Ps 77:12), on his precepts, decrees, and promises (Ps 119). Through meditation we become acquainted with God's character, intentions, and desires for all of his creation. Our entire being begins to pulsate with the heartbeat of God so that his ways become our ways not only outwardly through acts of compassion but inwardly through the transformation of our mind. In turn, this changes the structures of our brain by strengthening the synaptic connections of our altruistic brain so as to reflect the very nature of the compassionate heart of God.

The practice of meditation involves two types of attention, namely focused attention and bare attention.[60] Focused attention, as the name implies, is about directing unreservedly one's awareness onto a single object to the exclusion of everything else. Focused breathing, which is integral to all forms of meditation and relaxation exercises, is an example of this type of invested attention. It may also take the form of meditating on a particular verse (e.g., Col 3:12, "Therefore, as God's chosen people, holy and dearly loved, clothe yourselves with compassion, kindness, humility, gentleness and patience"). Bare or panoramic attention is more expansive in orienta-

58. Siegel, *The Mindful Brain*, 181.
59. Nolasco, *The Contemplative Counselor*, 45.
60. Ibid., 77.

tion as it stretches its gaze evenly on not just one object but on everything that comes in the field of perception.[61] An example would be to draw one's attention to the plight of those marginalized by church and society (e.g., victims of otherization) and to become aware both of the interlocking narratives and power structures that induce suffering and pain as well as subversive stories that break down the divide through acts of compassion. Both types of attention can induce or strengthen neural circuitry associated with our innate capacity for empathy and compassion.

The ability to direct our attention to single or multiple objects is primarily due to our asymmetrical bihemispheric brain. The left hemisphere is primed to have a narrow focused attention while the right hemisphere yields a broad vigilant attention.[62] The two types of attention when used singly or interchangeably during the practice of meditation have the potential to forge stronger connections between the two hemispheres of our brain. This "bilateral (cross-hemisphere) integration . . . would result in a more flexible, adaptive, coherent, energized, and stable state,"[63] which includes critical attitudes when engaged in the alleviation and transformation of the suffering of others.

A specific form of meditation that bears the fruit of neuroplasticity is mindfulness, a critical ingredient when cultivating compassion. To be mindful is to "become completely alive and live deeply each moment of daily life. Mindfulness helps you to touch the wonders of life for self-nourishment and healing. It also helps you to embrace and transform your afflictions into joy and freedom."[64] It means approaching life with intentionality and hospitable attention to the richness and poverty, profundity and simplicity, pain and joy of our life as it blossoms right now, in this sacred moment.[65]

The cultivation of mindfulness entails being aware of and attentive to the textured quality of human experience: the bodily sensations, states of mind, or the flow of thoughts and emotions as they surface in one's consciousness with an attitude of nonjudgment and acceptance, of letting things be as they are. It does not shy away from the reality of human suffering. As said previously, suffering is an inevitable aspect of the human

61. Ibid., 78.

62. McGilchrist, *The Master and His Emissary*, 27.

63. Siegel, *The Mindful Brain*, 226.

64. Thich Nhat Hahn, *Going Home*, 84.

65. Nolasco, *The Contemplative Counselor*, 40.

condition. It is to be expected and acknowledged but with the confidence that it can be alleviated and transformed. Compassionate love is understood as the crucial starting point for dealing with human suffering, which is made manifest by God himself through the example of Jesus Christ. Contemplating God's ever-expanding compassionate heart compels us to face suffering not with timidity but with great courage, confidence, and hope.[66]

In other words, as a form of Christian meditation, mindfulness heightens our ability to see beyond the external and into the inner divine life that is always present in us, inspiring us to be transformed into the likeness of Jesus Christ. Having the mind of Christ or imitating Christ in all aspects of our life is a clear expression of the presence of the divine life within us. St. John of the Cross echoes the same conviction when he says "those who take the spiritual seriously should be persuaded that the road leading to God does not require many considerations, methods, or unusual or extraordinary experiences . . . but one thing is necessary—self-denial and self-surrender for Christ's sake. All virtue is contained in this."[67] The graced disavowal of our lust for self-assertion and graced movement towards others through engaged compassion is an act of obedience to God, who calls us to have the same mind as Christ "who being in the very nature of God did not consider equality with God something to be grasped, but made himself nothing, taking the very nature of servant, being made in human likeness" (Phil 2:6–7).

Given the daily call for the renewal of our mind so that it becomes sensitive to the compassionate ways of God and responsive to the suffering of those around us and given the plasticity of the brain to represent on a neuronal level and mediate acts of altruistic love, we propose a series of meditation called the compassion cultivation training program. It will help bring compassion to everyday life. This program, which is discussed in detail in the next chapter, is inspired by the work of the Center for Compassion and Altruism Research and Education and yet differs significantly from it because of its religious orientation and foundation. However, though the entry point is different the ultimate goal remains the same, that is, to nourish a life of compassion as a loving response to human suffering. For the Christian, the cultivation of compassion is a way of inhabiting the mind of Christ that seeks to serve the interest of others, especially those who are pricked by life's thorns and thistles. It is a way of mediating the

66. Ibid.
67. John of the Cross, *The Ascent of Mount Carmel and the Dark Night*, 54.

presence of God in the midst of a hurting and suffering world, and through it we embody Immanuel—God with us!

Chapter Five

Cultivating Compassion

Setting the Context

The allure of the digital and consumerist age can be so irresistible at times, we can't help but buy into its promise of instant popularity and false intimacy. With a few snaps and clicks on our smart phones we amass images and tweets and then curate them for endless exhibition. Yet in the midst of excess and easy access to our personal lives we remain cut off from the depths of our heart and we feel so disoriented we miss the gift of the present moment. The longing for unconditional love and authentic existence and for a life with purpose and meaning that echoes deep within becomes a faint whisper that lingers outside of our awareness.

Sometimes though, this gentle whisper catches our attention and nudges us to listen to that still small voice inviting us to descend into the inner chambers of our heart where God watches, waits, and longs to be in communion with us. Indeed, there lies in all of us the seed of contemplation ready to be unearthed and nourished. Contemplation is about a "life in communion with God, an experienced union with the divine that yields the fruit of a transformed life that is fully awake and fully alive."[1] It is a gift graciously bestowed upon us because of our creatureliness as image-bearers of God that must then be received and nurtured so that it can be offered to others through a life of self-transcendence and service.

Contemplation is a way of knowing God and a way of being that mirrors Christ, who is the perfect image of the invisible God, in all of life. As a way of knowing, contemplation is characterized by "self forgetting

1. Nolasco, *The Contemplative Counselor*, 35.

attention, a humble receptiveness, a still and steady gazing, an intense concentration so that emotion, will and thought are all fused and lost in God who embraces them all. Gradually, by a deeper and deeper process of self-merging, a communion is established between the seer and what is seen, a communion is established between him [sic] who feels and that which he feels."[2] In this graced experience, we quiet all mental activities and in stillness and silence draw a loving attention toward our self-revealing God. We lay bare our hearts and strip ourselves of any desires or concerns of earthly life and in humility and deep gratitude surrender to the loving embrace of God who accepts us unreservedly just as we are. In that moment of stillness and quiet embrace we experience the generosity of God who offers a "glimpse of His majesty to the spirits of His servants,"[3] and an outpouring of love that knows no bounds.

As a way of being, contemplation quickens in us the desire to ascend from the sweetness of our union with God and into a life energized to love and serve others. In others words, in contemplation the experience of communion inevitably leads to a life of compassion. In some ways, this movement of descending into silence and solitude to be with God alone and ascending into service of others mirrors the very rhythm of Christ's life and ministry. This spiritual rhythm that contemplation arouses in us progressively transforms us into the likeness of Christ (2 Cor 3:18) and renews us so that we can have the mind of Christ (Phil 2:6–7). In the fusion of the human and the divine we begin to see clearly "who we truly are, who we always were, and this seeing helps us claim our deepest truth,"[4] that we truly are God's beloved whose nature and calling is to embody compassionate love.

Sadly, the onslaught of noise that assails us, coupled with our own proclivity for nonstop action, often deters us from inhabiting this spacious feeling of loving attention to God and attunement to the suffering of others. Consequently, we become mindless wanderers impulsively reacting to whatever will fancy our appetites and imagination, and our view turns myopic as we see nothing but ourselves stationed in and commanding the world of our own making. The "me first mentality" kicks in and it overshadows and obscures the "we belong sensibility." And when that happens we alienate ourselves from God's invitation for radical intimacy and forget that

2. Happold, *Mysticism*, 70.

3. Baker, "Sancta Sophia," 326.

4. Pierce, *We Walk the Path Together*, 97.

the suffering of another and the healing and transformation of that suffering are intricately intertwined with every fabric of our being.

Yet, amidst all this, there remains an open invitation for us to dwell in the presence of God (Ps 27:4). The sublime gift of contemplation "opens a door into this life of faith and authentic existence"[5] and it is always there for the taking. All that is needed is a humble acceptance of this gift and a commitment to nourish it so as to bear fruit of abiding communion and engaged compassion. But such acceptance requires awareness of and attention to that still gentle voice, which can be harnessed through the practice of mindfulness.

Mindfulness, as discussed in the previous chapter, is the capacity to inhabit the present moment in all its fullness with an attitude of hospitality and curiosity. It connects us deeply into our interior life by being mindful of our subjective thoughts and feelings as they surface in our consciousness and connects us profoundly to the external world to which we also are intimately linked or intertwined. Being mindfully aware, attuned, and accepting of what unfolds in the present moment allows us to feel more alive and genuinely engaged with life, with more depth and discernment.

The spacious quality of the heart that mindfulness nurtures creates many a room for others to dwell in. It trains the mind to give full and loving attention to the sweet whispers of God and heartfelt cries of those around us. Through mindfulness we become acutely aware of the suffering that is all around us, especially our role both in its course as well as its transformation. We cease to become bystanders detached and unaffected by the suffering of others. Instead, the gift of mindfulness allows us to look deeply into human suffering and to live purposely by participating in its healing.

Mindfulness also brings a sense of well being to the person practicing it. Since awareness and attention are operations of the brain and therefore activate neural circuitry they can "strengthen the synaptic linkages" in areas of the brain that bring well-being.[6] Research shows that those who are engaged in mindfulness practices report positive physical and psychological outcomes such as lowered blood pressure and reduction in emotional reactivity.[7] It has also been linked to the activation of the mirror neuron

---

5. Nolasco, *The Compassionate Counselor*, 40.

6. Siegel, *The Mindful Brain*, 31.

7. Kabat-Zinn, *Full Catastrophe Living*, 29–30.

system, which is the social circuitry responsible for interpersonal attunement via increased levels of empathy and compassion towards others.[8]

EXERCISE ONE: MINDFUL HEART AND MIND

Mindfulness and Contemplative Practice

The cultivation of contemplation and mindfulness begins with a very simple practice called Listening Exercise.[9]

Listening Exercise

- Sit in a comfortable chair in a quiet space, eyes either slightly open or gently closed.
- Place your hands on your lap with your palms facing up.
- Take a few deep breaths.
- Become mindful or aware of the air that is coming into and going out of your body, of your chest rising during the in-breath and collapsing on the out-breath. Linger here for a moment.
- Notice the sounds you hear about you. Listen first for the fainter, more distant sounds like the traffic, the wind blowing, rain dripping, air conditioning or heater buzzing, or people chattering, and just listen to these sounds as they are.
- Then listen to the sounds that are nearby. Again, simply become aware of them. Continue to breathe mindfully.
- Now draw your attention to your heart. Attend lovingly to the sound of your heartbeat, while you breathe mindfully.
- Notice the deepening sound of silence in this place of prayer.

8. Siegel, *The Mindful Brain*, 181.
9. Nolasco, *The Compassionate Counselor*, 116.

- Listen to the words of the Lord saying, "Be still and know that I am God." Linger here for a moment and let these words fill every part of your body.

- If your mind wanders—no problem, no judgment, and no shame. Just gently bring your attention back to the sensation of breathing and then rest in the promise of God's loving accompaniment with you in this present moment.

- When ready to come out of this silence, take a deep breath and open your eyes if they have been closed. Extend this focused attention and your consent to God's invitation for communion into your next activity and through the rest of the day.

For beginners, this basic mindfulness practice may feel quite challenging at first. Hence, it is quite normal to feel awkward, distracted, and unsettled at the beginning of the practice. We are constantly besieged by life's demands and pressures that in turn make it difficult for us to simply stop, pause, and catch our breath. Even in Christian circles and gatherings the rhythm is often busy, filled with gestures and voices, with little or no time for silence. In other words, the mindful practice of listening is counterintuitive at least in relation to the larger cultural injunction to stay busy and fill our lives with nonstop activity. All this is to say that in the first try of the listening exercise the struggle to stay attentive and focused is not only inevitable but to be anticipated.

At the same time, it is important to start developing an attitude of nonjudgment and curiosity when our mind wanders off during the exercise. The attitude of nonjudgment allows us to persevere in the midst of the difficulty to stay in the moment by normalizing and reframing it as germane to the development of being mindful. In fact, noticing the chatter of the mind during the exercise already indicates a blossoming of this capacity. As the exercise graciously reminds us, there is no judgment, no shame, and it is not a problem when we veer off course. Just simply notice the wandering and then gently return the attention back to breathing. Nurturing an attitude of curiosity, especially when struggling to stay in the moment, is equally important. This more hospitable and receptive stance to the experience creates an opening or invitation to understand more deeply the source or cause of the struggle. It will also expand our level of self-awareness especially, when we discover where our mind usually goes and the kinds of thoughts or messages we tell ourselves. The insight that is gained through the curious reflection of the experience could be a source of encouragement to habituate mindfulness.

It would be good to start in small increments and build from there. A regular five-minute daily practice of listening exercise in the morning before one is caught up with the activities of the day and another round just before one retires for the night may prove to be practically achievable. And for any habit to take root it must be patiently cultivated and practiced until it becomes second nature to us. It might also be helpful to remember not get fixated on the outcome, however good or beneficial that might be. As they say, the journey is as important as the destination, hence, try to commit to a daily practice and let the outcome be a welcome and wonderful revelation naturally flowing out of the mindfulness exercise itself.

As we lay the foundation of deep and mindful listening and notice the calming, expansive, and enlivening fruits it brings we can now challenge ourselves to carve out an extended time of twenty minutes for mindfulness meditation in the morning and evening. A lengthier time of regular prac-tice every day will create and sustain a deeper impression on our neural circuitry as well as in our mental and devotional life. The twenty-minute mindful meditation in the morning is our way of grounding ourselves to the challenges that lie ahead. This will prepare us to be less emotionally reactive to the day's twists and turns, more emotionally engaged and pres-ent with others and the work of our hands, and spiritually attuned to divine stirrings and inspirations. Below is a sample of an extended morning mind-fulness meditation practice.

Morning Mindfulness Meditation

- Sit in a comfortable chair in a quiet space, eyes either slightly open or gently closed.

- Place your hands on your lap with your palms facing up.

- Take a few deep breaths.

- Become mindful or aware of the air that is coming into and going out of your body, of your chest rising during the in-breath and collapsing on the out-breath. Linger here for a moment.

- Now bring to mind a layout of your day—tasks that need to be carried out, people to connect with, and other activities that need your careful attention, whether significant or trivial, one by one. Simply become aware of them and as best as you can refrain from strategizing or planning how you will approach these activities.

- Whenever you find yourself getting lost in your head or getting overwhelmed—no problem, no judgment, no shame. Gently draw your attention back to the sensation of breathing.

- As you begin to settle in your breathing once more, become aware of feelings, bodily sensations, and thoughts that begin to emerge. Treat them like clouds passing by your consciousness or purview waiting to be acknowledged but not analyzed. Label these feelings, name these thoughts, locate where this bodily sensations are coming from.

- In your in-breath say "I am" and in your out-breath name the feeling, thought, or sensation. Linger here for a moment until all the emergent feelings, thoughts, and sensations are labeled and breathed through.

- Gather all this—the schedule of day and the attendant states of mind—and imagine laying them down at the altar of grace (or foot of the cross) as an offering.

- In a posture of prayer incline the ears of your heart eager to listen to these words—"In all your ways acknowledge him and he will make your paths straight" (Prov 3:6). With a half-smile linger here for a moment and let these words permeate your consciousness and your entire being.

- In the last few minutes, take a few deep breaths and turn your attention again to the sensation of your breathing. When ready you can open your eyes if they have been closed and gradually engage the next activity with heartfelt intention and attention.

The twenty-minute mindful meditation in the evening may serve as a way of slowing down, reflecting back on the day's events, and purging ourselves of anything that may rob us of the peace and quiet so integral to a restful and relaxing sleep. A gesture of gratitude can also be included during this time of meditation. Below is a guided evening mindfulness meditation practice.

Evening Mindfulness Meditation

- Sit in a comfortable chair in a quiet space, eyes either slightly open or gently closed.

- Place your hands on your lap with your palms facing up.

- Take a few deep breaths.

- Become mindful or aware of the air that is coming into and going out of your body, of your chest rising during the in-breath and collapsing on the out-breath. Linger here for a moment.

- Now one by one bring to mind events that happened that day, whether salient or ordinary, positive or negative, as each emerges in your consciousness.

- Simply become aware of them. Continue to breathe mindfully as you try to remember the day's happenings.

- Whenever you find yourself getting lost in your head or you start saying things like "I could have, should have, would have"; no problem, no judgment, no shame. Acknowledge this thought pattern and then with a half-smile bring your attention back to the sensation of breathing.

- As you begin to settle in again, become aware of feelings, bodily sensations, and thoughts that begin to emerge as you recollect. Again, treat them like clouds passing by your consciousness or purview waiting to be acknowledged but not analyzed. Label these feelings, name these thoughts, locate where these bodily sensations are coming from.

- In your in-breath say "I am" and in your out-breath name the feeling, thought, or sensation. Linger here for a moment until all the emergent feelings, thoughts, and sensations are labeled and breathed through.

- Gather all this—the memories of the day with the attendant feelings, thought, and sensations—and imagine putting them all in the palm of your hand and blowing them gently into the wind.

- In a posture of prayer incline the ear of your heart eager to listen to these words—"Be anxious for nothing, but in everything by prayer and supplication with thanksgiving let your requests be made known to God" (Phil 4:6). Alternately, a verse of thanksgiving can be used as well—"I will give thanks to You, O Lord my God, with all my heart.

And I will glorify your name forever" (Ps 86:12). With a half-smile linger here for a moment and let these words permeate your consciousness and your entire being.

- In the last few minutes, take a few deep breaths and turn your attention again to the sensation of your breathing. When ready you can open your eyes if they have been closed and gradually engage the next activity with heartfelt intention, attention, and deep gratitude.

As a complement to this practice and to further deepen self-awareness set aside some time immediately after the exercise to reflect and write down your experiences, especially those feelings and thoughts that are recurring or needing further exploration with someone (e.g., a significant other, friend, therapist, spiritual director, pastor, fellow meditator). Though the practice itself is often singular the journey as a whole is communal. This conversation, either formally in therapy or informally with a partner, may assist in fostering self-understanding, accountability, intimacy, and communion with others. Since the mindfulness practice itself nurtures internal stability, coherence, and kindness to oneself we can approach this conversation, however painful or difficult it may seem, with equanimity and openness to the gift of healing it may bring.

A Prelude

The daily and personal practice of mindfulness is a prelude to subsequent compassion-focused meditative exercises. It prepares heart and mind to stay awake, alert, and attentive to the suffering of others and nurtures empathy and abiding connection with them as our fellow human beings. Devotionally, it also prepares our heart and mind to be indwelt by the Spirit of God through divine self-revelation through his Word and works in the world. This daily rhythm of surrender to God's compassionate ways renews our mind so that we can have the mind of Christ infusing all that we are and all that we do.

The focused attention we lay on our interiority and interaction with the external world also strengthens our capacity for bare or panoramic attention. As another form of attention our vision expands and is "flexible with whatever is in the field of perception."[10] Here we witness and give sustained and careful attention to interlocking variables—from personal

10. Speeth, "On Psychotherapeutic Attention," 153.

to social, religious to political, cultural to global—that influence people's behavior and experience in the world, particularly those that contribute to and alleviate human suffering. Bare attention with its emphasis on "impartiality, spaciousness, and breadth of vision"[11] evokes freedom and flexibility as well in discerning the best possible way of extending compassion to those in need.

. . . .

EXERCISE TWO: COMPASSIONATE HEART OF GOD

Setting the Context

"Behold, the virgin shall be with child and shall bear a Son, and they shall call his name Immanuel," which translated means, "God with us" (Matt 1:23). In this short rendering we witness a crisp yet profound description of the identity of Jesus Christ and the purpose of his incarnation. For this exercise our focus is on deepening our understanding of "God's with-ing" as an act of solidarity with the suffering of humanity. Jesus Christ as Immanuel is God's concrete, visible, and radical act of compassionate love in the face of human suffering.

Recall Jesus' encounter with a leper in Mark 1:41–42. Deformed in all sorts of ways and ostracized by people around him, the leper "knelt down and begged" Jesus to "make him clean" (v. 40). This heartfelt request that bubbled up from a place of incalculable pain and suffering and the posture of humility, reverence, and submission the leper showed evoked a response of "God's with-ing" captured in the phrase "[Christ was] moved with compassion" (v. 41). From our word study of compassion in Chapter 3 we discover that its Greek counterpart *splangchnizomai* means the entrails of the body. In lay parlance and in this context Jesus had a strong and intense gut reaction welling up from within. The sight of this suffering man moved the core of his body and touched his heart and mind so deeply it caused him to act—with much empathy and compassion. He "stretched out his hand and touched the leper" and by the power of his word the "leprosy left and

11. Ibid., 151.

he was cleansed" (v. 42). There is no grave disease or condition, physical or otherwise, that is beyond the reach of Christ's compassionate love. There is nothing that can deter him from entering into human pain and out of this "divine solidarity comes new life."[12]

In a similar demonstration of "God's with-ing" we witness Jesus Christ being "moved by compassion" when he saw a multitude of people "because they were like sheep without a shepherd" (Mark 6:33–35). Their predicament did not go unnoticed. Their weary and dispirited state tugged at Christ's tender heartstrings, as it were. He saw right through them, sensed what they needed, and met them in the most personal and loving manner—by teaching and then feeding them. As discussed earlier, the Hebrew word for compassion is *rachamin,* which means "the womb of Yahweh." In this narrative, Christ's compassion is like that of a mother protecting and nourishing her children not only with food but also with a steadfast promise and expression of tender loving care and presence, of "with-ing" especially during times of great need.

We all have been visited by suffering in all its forms—from physical to relational, from psychological to spiritual. Our body is weakened by disease, our relationships torn apart by wrong choices and missed opportunities, our self-worth and confidence shattered by dark shadows of a painful past, and our faith tested by an acute sense of God's absence. No matter the cause of suffering the impact seems to be the same—it is isolating, excruciatingly painful, even senseless and random at times.

Like the leper in the narrative we often find ourselves pleading earnestly for God to intervene, to heal our broken selves and relationships, to take us out of darkness and into the light of peace, joy, and a sense of well-being. Or like the throng people who followed and surrounded Christ our countenance may reveal a deep desire for rest and nourishment from a life that is adrift, disoriented, marked with scarcity, hunger, and thirst of all kinds. No matter the ache of our heart God is with us, his compassion is assured, and his accompaniment during times of turmoil and hardship is steadfast and secure.

The face of this compassion may vary—some of us may obtain healing and restoration, while others may be strengthened and their faith firmly rooted to withstand pain and suffering. However this face is shown upon us, however the compassionate presence of God is made manifest only one thing is for certain—God is with us and in that "with-ing" God made a

12. Nouwen et al., *Compassion,* 16.

"commitment to live in solidarity with us, to share our joys and pains, to defend and protect us, and to suffer all of life with us."[13] The greatest miracle is not the healing and the cure! It is the incarnation of God in Christ, the "Word who became flesh and dwelt among us" (John 1:14) and made himself vulnerable to pain and suffering so that he can enter into our own pain with loving-kindness and compassion. This extravagant display and gesture of divine love, intimacy and solidarity is vividly expressed in Isaiah 53:3–6:

> He was despised and rejected by mankind, a man of suffering, and familiar with pain. Like one from whom people hide their faces he was despised, and we held him in low esteem. Surely he took up our pain and bore our suffering yet we considered him punished by God, stricken by him and afflicted. But he was pierced for our transgressions; he was crushed for our iniquities; the punishment that brought us peace was on him, and by his wounds we are healed. We all, like sheep, have gone astray, each of us has turned to our own way; and the Lord has laid on him the iniquity of us all.

God knows our suffering! God shares our pain and sorrow and participates in our struggles! God has taken upon himself our iniquity and granted us healing for no other reason except love. His "with-ing" springs from the deep well of compassion that reaches out and embraces all suffering in order to transform it and to give witness to the "beautiful fruits of solidarity with our condition."[14] Hence, we come before God to receive this divine compassion freely offered to us unmerited and unbounded.

Receiving God's Compassion Meditation

- Sit in a comfortable chair in a quiet space, eyes either slightly open or gently closed.

- Place your hands on your lap with your palms facing up.

- Take a few deep breaths.

- Become mindful or aware of the air that is coming into and going out of your body, of your chest rising during the in-breath and collapsing on the out-breath. Linger here for a moment.

13. Ibid., 13.
14. Ibid., 16.

- Whenever you find yourself getting lost in your head or getting overwhelmed, no problem, no judgment, no shame. Gently draw your attention back to the sensation of breathing.

- Now picture yourself in the crowd whom Jesus saw and felt compassion towards. Notice his face, his eyes, and imagine him walking towards you. You feel his tenderness, warmth, and open stance. You experience his nearness and the assurance that he is there with you, so eager to touch and heal your aching heart, stifled spirit, distressed body, and broken relationships.

- While continuing to breathe mindfully, you hear the words of Christ—"Come to me all of you who are weary and I will give you rest" (Matt 11:28). Linger here for a moment and internalize the words spoken to you so lovingly and caringly.

- As you consent to this invitation you become aware of aspects of your life that need the compassionate touch of God. Name them one by one and offer them up to God in humility, reverence, and submission.

- Let the warmth of God's compassion lift your burdens up to make you feel light, accompanied, strengthened, and assured. With a half-smile linger here for a moment and try to immerse yourself fully into this experience of God's "with-ing" amidst your suffering and in the concreteness of your life.

- In the last few minutes, take a few deep breaths and turn your attention again to the sensation of your breathing. When ready you can open your eyes if they have been closed and direct a loving gaze outward and into the rest of your day.

The above meditation, like the previous ones and those following, can be done in small groups, perhaps with minor alterations to fit the unique context of the gathered community. To maximize the benefit of this group experience it is best to set aside a time for shared reflection. The following guided questions may help spur the beginning of a meaningful conversation.

1. How did you experience the meditation?

2. What thoughts, feelings, and bodily sensations came up for you when you visualized Christ coming towards you with warmth, tenderness, and compassion?

CULTIVATING COMPASSION

3. What is it like to receive God's compassion and invitation to rest in him?

4. What thoughts, feelings, and sensations did you become aware of when you named your suffering? How about the moment when you surrendered it to God?

5. What has been the most challenging aspect of this meditation? What has been the most enriching part of this experience?

An attitude of hospitality and curiosity must pervade this conversation. There are no right or wrong answers to these questions. There are no good or bad meditators, just difference in the ability to stay focused and attentive, which can be harnessed through regular practice and perseverance. During this time of sitting together we aim for an authentic sharing and acceptance of truth discovered during the meditative experience. In this atmosphere of mutual exchange the isolation that suffering brings dissolves in the presence of the accompaniment of others. By listening deeply to the stories of others we become aware not only of our differences but our common humanity as well and together we experience the in-breaking of God-with-us whose compassion is offered to us all.

EXERCISE THREE: SELF-COMPASSION

Setting the Context

Jules showed up for supervision very composed but somewhat dispassionate. Her demeanor was guarded, her responses brief, and her facial expression impassive. After a short exchange of pleasantries and a brief overview of our time together Jules's tough exterior began to crumble. Her hands started to shake and her breathing became short and shallow. Noticing this quick change in her behavior I invited her to take a few deep breaths and then guided her through a short mindfulness exercise. After she regained her composure she started to share how anxious she has been leading up to our supervision. She disclosed her deep-seated fear of failure and how she thought that her videotaped counseling session would confirm what she already knew about herself all along—that she was not good enough to be a counselor. Such feeling of inadequacy is not alien to Jules and it tends to rear its ugly head when her performance or work is evaluated. Admittedly, this is an area that Jules has been working through in her personal therapy.

To her supervisor, though, Jules has already shown great potential as a counselor. Her sessions are marked with careful execution of basic counseling skills and her relational stance towards her client is very inviting, non-threatening, and safe. These, among others, have been highlighted during supervision, which provided some relief from this ongoing struggle of self-doubt. Like most people, the conflict between self-perception (i.e., Jules sees her self as inadequate) and other-perception (i.e., faculty and peers see her potential) stems from a life experience that is filled with criticism, judgment, and negative messaging by self and others, usually familial and those in close relationships. And despite evidence to the contrary and the psychological damage it inflicts, individuals like Jules tend to listen more and put great import towards the critical voice that runs ceaselessly in the background.

Raiff is a mid-level manager in one of the big telecommunication companies in town. He is well-spoken, takes pride in his job, and very determined to climb the corporate ladder. Over the years, he has learned to sacrifice his personal life in favor of a promising career, which means long hours at work and professional access through his cell phone even on weekends. Expectedly, this has taken a toll on him in all ways possible. He is increasingly becoming impatient and easily angered by any slight misstep at work, disagreements with his colleagues, and the onslaught of demands and pressures at home. Raiff is on the "brink of exploding" and he has sought therapy to help him deal with "anger issues."

As our therapeutic work progressed Raiff discovered an aspect of himself that he had long tried to hide and keep at bay—that is, his sense of worth is linked to his work. Consequently, anything that resembles criticism with regards to his work performance elicits a quick defensive reaction as he takes it as an attack on his personhood. Anger acts as a shield against the arrows of doubt, either self-induced or intimated by others, that come his way and pierce his insecure self. Much to his chagrin these angry outbursts are becoming more frequent, which inevitably creates stress and tension in his personal and professional life. To mitigate further damage therapy entailed more than just "anger management" to include an exploration of a territory quite unfamiliar to him—a path towards self-acceptance where worth is based not on performance but on his revered stature simply as a human being.

The stories of Jules and Raiff are far too common and their trajectories are awfully predictable. The familiar script of insecurity and self-loathing that animates these stories is often hidden under the guise of human strivings for perfection and relentless pursuit to be successful. In some cases, this subtext is not easily concealed and gives way to pride, self-aggrandizement, hatred, and diminishment of others. What we resist acknowledging in ourselves persists and gets projected onto others—a mechanism that underlies negative behaviors and attitudes towards others, leading to various expressions of otherization.

Like any edifice that has a weak foundation, this carefully built defensive fortress will collapse and become a wasteland of suffering littered with depression, anxiety, addictions, and violence against others. But the story line does not have to end this way since their suffering can be ameliorated by having a different attitude towards themselves. In other words, the fractured self that is at the core of these narratives can be mended and made whole again.

The process of transformation begins where the problem lies—in the self. Only this time, the self is treated with kindness and compassion and not with judgment and negative appraisals. The attitude of self-compassion is composed of three related components: "1) self-kindness—being kind and understanding toward oneself in instances of pain or failure rather than being harshly self-critical; 2) common humanity—perceiving one's experiences as part of the larger human experience rather than seeing them as separating and isolating; 3) mindfulness—holding painful thoughts and feelings in balanced awareness rather than over-identifying with them."[15] These components are already present in the first two mindfulness exercises discussed above. In other words, the groundwork for a more kind and compassionate stance towards self has already been laid and must be cultivated regularly to bear the fruits of compassion.

• For many a Christian, the root of self-compassion is the experience of receiving God's compassionate love towards us, with the divine image deeply etched in all of us. This loving and experiential knowledge of a compassionate God makes possible an identity that is graced, acquired not on merit or good works but on our status as God's own beloved. And the "closer we move towards the heart of God the more we realize, and embrace

15. Neff, Self-Compassion, 41.

the profound truth that we are deeply loved just as we are."[16] There is no amount of human strivings or human failings that can alter God's unconditional love towards us. Hence, we no longer have to run away from or conceal our wounded and fragile self. We need not wear a mask of unyielding self-belief or regard ourselves as better than others. God's acceptance of us just as we are empowers us to accept ourselves as we are. By confronting our own adversity with the eyes of a loving, compassionate God we realize that the "power to heal comes from the transformation of vulnerability into sensitivity, vision, and compassion."[17] Here again, we see the power of God's "with-ing" in enabling us to stay with our pain and suffering and through that accompaniment and balanced awareness of our condition we experience a kinder, more compassionate version of ourselves that lies within. •

Self-Compassion Meditation

- Sit in a comfortable chair in a quiet space, eyes either slightly open or gently closed.

- Place your hands on your lap with your palms facing up.

- Take a few deep breaths.

- Become mindful or aware of the air that is coming into and going out of your body, of your chest rising during the in-breath and collapsing on the out-breath. Linger here for a moment.

- Whenever you find yourself getting lost in your head or getting overwhelmed, no problem, no judgment, no shame. Gently draw your attention back to the sensation of breathing.

- Now picture yourself in the crowd that Jesus saw and felt compassion towards. Notice his face, his eyes, and imagine him walking towards you. You feel his tenderness, warmth, and open stance. You experience his nearness and the assurance that he is there with you.

- While continuing to breathe mindfully, imagine offering jarred pieces of your broken self to Christ—your insecurity and fear of failure and rejection, your self-doubt and feeling of being unwanted, unloved, and not cared for.

16. Nolasco, *The Compassionate Counselor*, 22

17. Goldberg, *On Being a Psychotherapist*, 49.

- Notice how you feel when you surrender these broken pieces to God. Do you feel lighter, made whole, and loved unconditionally?

- As you gaze upon his face you hear the words—"I will give thanks to you, for I am delicately and wonderfully made. Wonderful are your works, and my soul knows it very well" (Ps 139:14).

- Now place your right hand on your heart while letting these words echo deep within. Lean into these words and notice how you feel. Do you feel any sensation? Do you feel deeply loved, cared for, accepted, and intimately close to the source of this love?

- If not, that is fine. No judgment, no problem, no shame. Just focus on the sensation of your breathing or the loving face of Christ or the words spoken earlier and breathe mindfully.

- With a half-smile silently recite to yourself the following phrase:

  "May I feel the love of Christ for me.
  May this love heal those broken pieces of myself and make me whole.
  May I know in my heart and mind that I am God's Beloved.
  That I am deeply loved just as I am."

- Breathe and silently repeat these words two more times. Linger here for a moment.

- Again, notice how this feels in your heart. Did you notice any change in how you feel and think about yourself? Are you beginning to see yourself the way God sees you? If so, bathe yourself in this intimate knowing that God loves you as you are.

- In the last few minutes, take a few deep breaths and turn your attention again to the sensation of your breathing. When ready you can open your eyes if they have been closed and direct a loving gaze outward and into the rest of your day.

• The internalization of God's compassion towards us rekindles the flame of self-compassion that has been flickering and waiting to be ignited. Extending and receiving care is innately human; it is part of our attachment and caregiving system, which has enabled us to survive and thrive. The above guided meditation exercise taps into this system and its attendant "chemicals of care"[18] like oxytocin (see Chapter 3) that when released

18. Neff, *Self-Compassion*, 47.

regularly results in a robust brain connections and healthy and nourishing interpersonal relations.

It is also worth mentioning that the cultivation of self-compassion does not eradicate the human tendency to feel unpleasant emotions like anger, anxiety, and fear. Our human condition makes us susceptible to suffering and with it are varied unpleasant emotions that may sometimes overwhelm us. However, with daily practice of compassion meditation we learn to respond and relate differently to these emotions and even use them skillfully to further our growth. After all, compassion "is not about ascent and moving above suffering, it is about descent into the grittiness of suffering . . . to hold [difficult emotions] in a compassionate space and to develop wisdom to know how to work with them."[19] But how does one work with emotions like anxiety or anger from a place of compassion? The following meditations target specifically these two emotions and make use of the gains achieved in previous mindfulness exercises.

Compassion for the Anxious Self

- Sit in a comfortable chair in a quiet space, eyes either slightly open or gently closed.

- Place your hands on your lap with your palms facing up.

- Take a few deep breaths.

- Become mindful or aware of the air that is coming into and going out of your body, of your chest rising during the in-breath and collapsing on the out-breath. Linger here for a moment.

- Whenever you find yourself getting lost in your head or getting overwhelmed, no problem, no judgment, no shame. Gently draw your attention back to the sensation of breathing.

- Get in touch with your compassionate self—the part of you that is secure and rooted in God's love for you, that reminds you of your belovedness despite your flaws and shortcomings. Identify with and lean into the innate qualities of your compassionate self—empathic, accepting, awake, benevolent especially in the face of suffering, and mindful at all times. Linger here for a moment until you experience the warm embrace of your compassionate self.

19. Gilbert and Choden, *Mindful Compassion,* 172.

- Now bring to mind a time when you were feeling anxious, tense, nervous, scared, or uneasy. Or if you are sensing those feelings right now, at this moment, that is all right, too. Just remember that you are looking at that anxious part of you through the eyes of your compassionate self.

- Give yourself permission to feel connected with that feeling of anxiety while you remain grounded in the qualities of your compassionate self. Try to locate that feeling in your body as you continue to breathe mindfully. Do you feel it in your chest, or shoulders, or stomach?

- Place your hand gently on that part of your body where you feel anxious as if cradling or soothing an agitated child. Then breathe through your anxiety gently, slowly, and with empathy.

- While remaining anchored in your compassionate self begin to think of the anxiety as a guest bearing a gift or a message. What does this feeling want you to know? What is this feeling needing from you? Validation? Understanding? Acknowledgement? Resolution? Whatever it is let the compassionate self be your guide as you deepen your awareness and understanding of this feeling.

- Now see yourself in your mind's eye and then with a half-smile offer these words to that part of you that feels anxious

    [Say your name], may you be free of anxiety.
    May you be free of worries and fears.
    May you experience the Peace of Christ that makes you well and whole.

    Say these words two more times, gently, slowly, expectantly, again letting compassion flow from your compassionate self to your anxious self. Linger here for moment while you breathe mindfully.

- Notice how this feels in your heart. Do you feel less anxious, light, at peace? If so, bathe yourself in this peaceful state. If not, that's all right, no judgment, no shame, and no problem. Just remain connected to your intention to be kind and compassionate to that part of you.

- In the last few minutes, take a few deep breaths and turn your attention again to the sensation of your breathing. When ready you can open your eyes if they have been closed and direct a loving gaze outward and let the peace radiate from the inside out.

The above meditation contains several features worth highlighting that may hopefully serve as a guidepost during the practice. First, it builds on the skills learned from the previous mindfulness and compassion meditation exercises. The burgeoning capacity to listen deeply, to focus our attention on an object like the breath, the nonjudgmental attitude that we bring to the practice, and the awareness of and consenting to God's invitation for communion and rest makes it easier to attend skillfully to such unpleasant emotions as anxiety. Second, connecting with our compassionate self provides stability, courage, empathy, and wisdom as we enter into and stay present to the anxious part of ourselves. In other words, it serves as an anchor as we weather the storm that swirls around in our emotional landscape. Third, locating where anxiety is lodged in our body indicates that emotions are more than just mental states and that our emotional system in our brain sends signals to the rest of our body so that we can deal with our situation more effectively.[20] The soft, caring, and empathic approach we bring to our emotions (i.e., placing our hand gently on that part of the body where we feel the emotion and treating it as an honored guest) affords us with numerous possibilities on how best to regulate them. Fourth, verbally wishing and praying for wellness and peace strengthens our intention or conviction to be kind and compassionate towards ourselves. The power of intention further cements our commitment to relate differently to aspects of ourselves that we tend to judge or be critical about. And lastly, the check-in that happens towards the end of the meditation is a way of mentalizing or naming the experience, of understanding and appreciating the experience whatever that might be. This capacity to mentalize yields fruits of flexibility, choice, and self-agency. All these principles apply to our next self-compassion meditation; only this time, the focus is on a different emotion—anger.

Compassion for the Angry Self

- Sit in a comfortable chair in a quiet space, eyes either slightly open or gently closed.
- Place your hands on your lap with your palms facing up.
- Take a few deep breaths.

---

20. Ellis, "Mapping emotions in the body yields consistent global results."

- Become mindful or aware of the air that is coming into and going out of your body, of your chest rising during the in-breath and collapsing on the out-breath. Linger here for a moment.

- Whenever you find yourself getting lost in your head or getting overwhelmed, no problem, no judgment, no shame. Simply and gently draw your attention back to the sensation of breathing.

- Get in touch with your compassionate self—the part of you that is secure and rooted in God's love for you, that reminds you of your belovedness despite your flaws and shortcomings. Identify with and lean into the innate qualities of your compassionate self—empathic, accepting, awake, benevolent—especially in the face of suffering—and mindful at all times. Linger here for a moment until you experience the warm embrace of your compassionate self.

- Now bring to mind a time when you were feeling angry, frustrated, annoyed, or irritable. Or if you are sensing those feelings right now, at this moment, that is alright too. Just remember that you are looking at anger through the eyes of your compassionate self. Then take a few deep breaths.

- Give yourself permission to feel connected with that feeling while you remain grounded in the qualities of your compassionate self. Try to locate that feeling in your body as you continue to breathe mindfully. How does anger feel in your mind and in your body? Do you feel it in your arms, chest, or head?

- Place your hand gently on that part of your body where you feel the anger as if cradling or soothing an agitated child. Then breathe through your anger gently, slowly, and with empathy.

- While remaining anchored in your compassionate self who sees your suffering begin to think of anger as a guest bearing a gift or a message. What does this feeling want you to know? What are you angry about? Is there an unmet need that you are protesting about—like the need for acceptance, love, understanding, inclusion, respect, to be seen or acknowledged, or cared for? Spend some time identifying this unmet need as you continue to breathe deeply.

- Also, are there other feelings that anger is trying to hide or cover—are there feelings of sadness, loss, fear, hurt, insecurity, or loneliness underneath the anger? Stay here for a moment and see if there's any other emotion beside the anger. Whatever it is try to get in touch with this feeling while simultaneously letting the compassionate self be your guide as you deepen your awareness and understanding of this feeling.

- Remember that your compassionate self recognizes what anger does to you and perhaps to people around you and it wants you to be freed from it. Your compassionate self is also able to contain this feeling and knows of its transient nature—that is, this feeling will come to pass and that you have the emotional strength to let anger move through you without being overwhelmed by it. You also have the emotional intelligence to deal with it constructively.

- Now see yourself in your mind's eye and then with a half-smile offer these words to that part of you that feels angry

  [Say your name], may you be free from the destructive effects of anger.
  May you have the wisdom to know the source of your anger and the feeling that lies underneath it.
  May you experience the Peace of Christ that makes you well and whole.

  Say these words two more times, gently, slowly, expectantly, again letting compassion flow from your compassionate self to your angry self. Linger here for moment while you breathe mindfully.

- Notice how this feels in your heart. Do you feel relaxed, grounded, and at peace? If so, bathe yourself in this peaceful state. If not, that's all right, no judgment, no shame, and no problem. Just remain connected to your intention to be kind and compassionate to that part of you.

- In the last few minutes, take a few deep breaths and turn your attention again to the sensation of your breathing. When ready you can open your eyes if they have been closed and direct a loving gaze outward and let the peace radiate from the inside out.

The ultimate goal of this meditation is to offer compassion to that part of ourselves that is angry. This stance is neither resisting or fighting against the emotion nor denying its existence. Instead, it creates a hospitable space where anger is felt, acknowledged or validated, and understood. Part of understanding this emotion is to detect any unmet need, where anger is used as a cry of protest, or any other emotion (e.g., sadness, hurt, fear, insecurity) that anger is covering. With compassion, we transform anger into something constructive—as a way of setting boundaries, of asserting our needs, and deepening our level of self-awareness and agency.

Like anxiety, anger can swiftly activate our limbic system and readies us to adopt a fight-or-flight defensive reaction. The above meditation taps into our soothing/caregiving system, which de-escalates the anger and heightens our ability to relate to it more healthily. Furthermore, we are also acutely aware that severe anxiety and anger that easily turns into rage can be debilitating and destructive on one's personal, relational, and occupational life. If that were the case, it would be important to seek the help of a professional and then use the above meditation as a supplemental resource.

Chapter Six

Extending Compassion

Setting the Context

Regular meditation taps into and harnesses the caregiving/nurturing emotional system in our brain, which in turn readies us to exhibit pro-social and affiliative behaviors towards others. The series of compassion meditation practices presented in the previous chapter release this capacity and make us more mindful, awake, and alert to the suffering of those around us. We become more sensitive to their anguish and cry for help, more empathic to their condition, and immensely interested and invested to help alleviate their suffering. The neural circuitry that underlies all this only proves again and again that we are wired for connection and compassion. It is deeply embedded into our brain structure and deeply etched into the very nature of what makes us human.

Compassion as neighborly love in action is also at the very heart of what it means to be a Christian and best offered as an expression of life together. Our religious life takes root in our fellowship with Christ who in turn initiates us into fellowship with other believers. Thus, a life of compassion characterizes the life of the community gathered around Christ who is the embodiment of God's compassionate heart. In our discussion of kenosis or self-emptying in Chapter 4, we discover that habituating the "mind of Christ" involves putting the needs of others above our own and in humility participating in their flourishing. The expression of compassionate love is not done in isolation but is pursued and made manifest within the context of community. The words of the Apostle Paul are instructive in this regard—"Therefore if you have any encouragement from being united with Christ, if any comfort for his love, if any common sharing in the Spirit, if any tenderness and compassion, then make my joy complete by being like-minded, having the same love, being one in spirit and of one mind" (Phil 1:1–2).

As a community of faith we reflect and mediate the presence of Christ by being "open and receptive to the suffering of the world and offer[ing] it a compassionate response."[1] This compassionate response is borne out of our mindful awareness of the ubiquitous nature of suffering and a hopeful stance that in the midst of these God remains with us and transforms us to be a people of God who offer "boundless compassion"[2] towards those acutely stricken by the finitude of the human condition. For whenever there are two or three gathered in the name of Christ (see Matt 18:20) compassion happens in the world and when it does we "participate in the divine compassion."[3]

Compassion as the fruit of our life together entails a commitment to "displacement and togetherness."[4] When God calls disparate individuals and forms them into a community under the Lordship of Christ they are "being-gathered-in-displacement,"[5] set apart for God, and are tasked to mediate God's presence in the midst of a broken world. This voluntary displacement takes us out of our familiar and comfortable worlds and into places and spaces where "people hurt and where we can experience with them our common human brokenness and our common need for healing."[6]

As we respond to God's call for displacement we partake and proclaim a new and radical way of being together.[7] Having been knitted together by the same Spirit (1 Cor 12:13) and having the same love, being one in spirit and of one mind (Phil 2:2), we begin to see each other and those around us the way God sees all of us—with love and compassion that knows no limits or conditions. Hence, our life together does not shy away from exposing our vulnerabilities and common humanity but confronts it with acceptance, grace, and an affirmation of our intrinsic value and worth. When it comes to embodying compassion no one is on the outside, indeed, God's

1. Nouwen et al., *Compassion*, 50.
2. Ibid., 54.
3. Ibid., 55.
4. Ibid., 59.
5. Ibid.
6. Ibid. 62.
7. Ibid., 74.

outstretched arms embrace the suffering of all. And God accomplishes this through the lives of those whom God has formed to be the body of Christ, the living witness to God's compassionate presence amidst a hurting world.

The series of meditations offered in this chapter flows out of this conviction. It starts with a compassion meditation for a loved one—a family member, a relative, or a dear friend—and then extends it beyond this inner circle. These are people whose lives are intertwined with ours, and whose presence brings comfort, assurance, and safety. But like the rest of us, they, too, are subject to the fragility of the human condition and therefore suffer in ways that are both familiar and strange to us. In certain cases, we are invited to share their pain by being vulnerable with them. And in others we can only infer their suffering from their sad or troubled faces, guarded movements, momentary withdrawal, irritability, or impatience. Given our physical and psychological proximity with our loved ones we can sense the ache of their soul and empathize with what they are going through. This meditative practice is a way of accompanying them through their darkest hour and our compassionate response brings a ray of light and hope.

These practices, like the previous ones, are meant to strengthen our resolve and commitment to live a life of compassion both in spirit and action. To forge the link between compassion and community life it might be beneficial to practice these meditations in small group settings. This shared experience connects one with the other on numerous levels. From a neurological vantage point, mirroring each other's intent to be compassionate strengthens our brain circuitry responsible for pro-social and affiliative behaviors. From a psychological perspective, this communal experience promotes healthy emotional bonds that are necessary so that the suffering of others are not carried alone but are shared by all. From a theological and spiritual viewpoint, when we engage in this experience we enter into fellowship with Christ and enter into a new relationship with each other.[8]

8. Ibid., 48.

EXERCISE FOUR: COMPASSION FOR A LOVED ONE

Compassion for a Loved One

- Sit in a comfortable chair in a quiet space, eyes either slightly open or gently closed.

- Place your hands on your lap with your palms facing up.

- Take a few deep breaths.

- Become mindful or aware of the air that is coming into and going out of your body, of your chest rising during the in-breath and collapsing on the out-breath. Linger here for a moment.

- Whenever you find yourself getting lost in your head or distracted, no problem, no judgment, no shame. Gently draw your attention back to the sensation of breathing.

- Bring to mind someone in your life today whom you feel very close to, supported and loved by deeply, who is suffering. It might help to remember a recent encounter with this person. What was he/she wearing? Where and when did you meet this person? As best as you can, imagine vividly his/her face, the tone of his/her voice, gestures, mannerisms, and demeanor.

- Notice how it feels in your heart when you bring this person's face right in your mind and heart. Do you feel warm, tender, and loving towards this person?

- Focus your attention on a time when your loved one shared with you (or that you sensed somehow) his/her suffering. It might be a struggle in the marriage, a challenging work situation, a health condition or sickness, worries or concerns about the children, or a troubled relationship with a friend or family member. Whatever the case may be, think of that time when this person was suffering and in pain. If you can, inhabit the world of this person and try to feel his/her pain, longing, sadness and sorrow, and the ache of his/her soul. Imagine what it would be like to be him/her at this moment in time, struggling and suffering beyond what he/she can bear. Breathe through those feelings, thoughts, and sensations that are bubbling up inside and let your breathing expand your empathy towards this person.

- Now imagine holding a lit candle that symbolizes Christ who is light and love and who cares deeply for the well being of your loved one. Offer this lighted candle to this person whom you love dearly and silently recite these words.

  May this light illumine and heal your pain and suffering.
  May you feel the compassionate presence of Christ in your life.
  May you have courage, grace, and peace.

- Breathe and silently repeat these words two more times. Again, notice how this feels in your heart when you bring this person's face in your mind and heart. Do you feel warm, tender, and loving towards this person?

- Think of concrete ways that you might want to consider doing to alleviate the suffering of your loved one. Might it be a visit, an email, text, or phone call, a meal to help ease his/her suffering? Whatever it is, allow your compassionate self to guide you in your efforts to bring relief to his/her suffering and commit yourself to doing this act of kindness.

- In the last few minutes, take a few deep breaths and turn your attention again to the sensation of your breathing. When ready you can open your eyes if they have been closed and direct a loving gaze outward and into the rest of your day.

. . . .

EXERCISE FIVE: COMPASSION FOR A NEIGHBOR

Setting the Context

For most of us our waking hours are spent interacting with diverse individuals on a regular basis either in the workplace or at school. In some cases we also meet and interact with other people rather informally at the supermarket and shopping malls, our favorite coffee shops, gyms, public transport, and churches.

These places are hubs for people who are going about their lives at a seemingly hurried pace, shuttling back and forth between commitments and burdened with life's demands and pressures. Driven as we are by a culture or a cult of busyness, getting out of this rat race mentality seems farfetched, especially when being busy is equated with being productive or when it affords us with self-importance. Hence, it is rather easy to live in our private worlds with little or no space left for others to be a part of it. Though we may see each other we fail to look deeply beyond what we see, we may hear words exchanged but fail to listen to their hidden meaning, we may talk to each other but fail to speak our heart's intent. In other words, we hide behind the veil of our busy and private worlds and therefore miss an opportunity to encounter the person behind the mask.

Recall once again the story of the Good Samaritan explored in Chapter 3, then place yourself in the narrative as one of the characters. Who among them can you identify with? How are we like the priest and the Levite who "passed on the other side" and ignored the suffering of another because we are too busy, too consumed, and too committed to our own agenda or to-do list? Who are the Good Samaritans in our lives who showed mercy and compassion during times of trouble and adversity? What is it like to be cared for lovingly by someone whom we barely know and whose generosity of time and resources relieved our own suffering? Conversely, how might we cultivate an attitude of neighborly love towards those whom we work with, or sit next to in class or at church, or those who provide "customer service" to ease the grind of daily living? How can we step out of our comfortable yet myopic world and become attentive to the inner turmoil that lurks behind the façade of these familiar faces we meet everyday?

The meditation offered here is a way of widening our circle of compassion to include these individuals who are in the web of relationships of which we are part. We may not be able to snatch them out of this hysteria that pervades our culture but we can relate to them with intentionality, engaging them as persons whose value and worth are based not on works or service but on them being a member of the human family. We may not be able to know intimately their stories but we can regard them as fellow sojourners walking on the same path towards a life that is flourishing and with purpose and meaning. We may not able to be there with them when they need immediate assistance and help but we can offer them peace and wish them well even from a distance. But when we are invited or have the opportunity to come alongside them during times of trouble and pain we don't hesitate, instead, we approach respectfully and offer acts of compassion with skill, discernment, and grace. This meditation harnesses this capacity to be mindful of those we meet on the road of life and offer them a compassionate presence that will hopefully break down barriers and build bridges of solidarity and hospitality.

Compassion for a Neighbor

- Sit in a comfortable chair in a quiet space, eyes either slightly open or gently closed.
- Place your hands on your lap with your palms facing up.
- Take a few deep breaths.
- Become mindful or aware of the air that is coming into and going out of your body, of your chest rising during the in-breath and collapsing on the out-breath. Linger here for a moment.
- Whenever you find yourself getting lost in your head or distracted, no problem, no judgment, and no shame. Gently draw your attention back to the sensation of breathing.
- Bring to mind someone whom you to interact with or meet on a regular basis—he/she could be a co-worker, a fellow student, a brother or sister in the Lord, a next-door neighbor, a person working in a coffee shop or supermarket. It might help to remember a recent encounter with this person. What was he/she wearing? Where and when did you meet this person? As best as you can, imagine vividly his/her face, the tone of his/her voice, gestures, mannerisms, and demeanor. And then simply offer these words of blessing for this person.

  May you be well, happy, and at peace.
  May you be free from pain and suffering.
  May you live your life with ease.

- Notice how it feels in your heart when you bring this person's face right into your mind and heart. Do you feel warm, tender, and kind towards this person?

- As well, recall a time when this same person (or someone else for that matter) has shared with you (or that you sensed somehow) his/her suffering. It might be a struggle in the marriage, a challenging work situation, a health condition or sickness, worries or concern about the children, a troubled relationship with a friend or family member. Whatever the case may be, think of that time when this person is suffering and in pain. If you can, inhabit the world of this person and try to feel his/her pain, longing, sadness and sorrow, and the ache of his/her soul. Imagine what it would be like to be him/her at this moment in time struggling and suffering beyond what he/she can bear. Breathe through those feelings, thoughts, and sensations that are bubbling up inside and let your breathing expand your empathy towards this person.

- Now imagine holding a lit candle that symbolizes Christ who is light and love and who cares deeply for the well-being of this person. Offer this lighted candle to him/her and then silently recite these words.

    May this light illumine and heal your pain and suffering.
    May you feel the compassionate presence of Christ in your life.
    May you have courage, grace, and peace.

- Breathe and silently repeat these words two more times. Again, notice how this feels in your heart when you bring this person's face into your mind and heart. Do you feel warm, tender, and kind towards this person?

- Think of concrete ways that you might want to do to alleviate the suffering of this person. Might a visit, an email, text, a phone call, or a meal to help ease his/her suffering? Whatever it is, allow your compassionate self to guide you in your efforts to bring relief to his/her suffering and commit yourself to doing this act of kindness.

- In the last few minutes, take a few deep breaths and turn your attention again to the sensation of your breathing. When ready you can open your eyes if they have been closed and direct a loving gaze outward and into the rest of your day.

EXERCISE SIX: COMPASSION FOR A CHALLENGING OTHER

Setting the Context

The suffering that we endure or witness around us originates from myriad forces—from those induced by human will (moral evil) and those caused by nature (natural evil). Each brings in its wake incalculable pain that often reduces their victims to tears of angry protest, anguish, and despair, especially when it is inflicted deliberately by a fellow human being. We have explored an aspect of moral evil in Chapter 2 that continues to taint and question the gospel of love that Christianity proclaims. Known as otherization, individuals who adhere to a belief system that conflict with the conservative or fundamentalist view are subjected to various forms of cruelty and violence. They are otherized or categorized as belonging to an "out-group" and therefore must be seen as a threat to the integrity of the "in-group." Efforts are then extended to exclude, separate, and even demonize those whom they believe to have strayed from the truth.

The process of otherization does not *just* happen to anyone or simply occur in isolation. As conveyed in earlier discussion, it is part of interlocking variables—from the personal (e.g., overestimation of self) to sociocultural (e.g., homophobic attitudes and practices) to religious (e.g., using the name of God to justify religious violence)—that purports to propagate a message of hate and exclusion towards those considered an "other." And unbeknownst to many, these negative and menacing messages tap into the primitive brain and trigger a fight-or-flight response as a way of warding off perceived or imagined threats. All these variables are intertwined so closely they co-opt each other and become a breeding ground for otherization. Inevitably, these inhumane attitudes and practices foment so much suffering that they cast much doubt, suspicion, anger, and disbelief regarding the truth claims of Christianity as a religion of love.

Thankfully, all these are reversible. The message of hate and exclusion can be supplanted by a message of compassion. The primitive brain that gets activated by repeated exposure to a threatening stimuli that is concocted based on fear, ignorance, desire for power and control, prejudice, and self-righteousness can be dampened by an equally powerful brain system of empathy and compassion that is innate in all of us. The church can once again be a refuge for those crushed or ravaged by human frailties and nature's wrath, a sacred space where compassion meets and transforms suffering. In this hallowed meeting, differing beliefs are acknowledged and respected and what takes center stage is an embodiment of compassionate presence that seeks to alleviate human suffering of all kinds.

How might we turn the tide of exclusion that drowns the humanity of those otherized and draw them to the wellspring of compassionate love where their humanity is restored, honored, and celebrated? There is no other place to start this journey than the human heart and mind and no better place to gain support, encouragement, and inspiration than the community of believers constituted by the God who abounds in love and compassion. But it takes courage, hospitality, and discipline to subvert the dehumanizing effects of otherization and reverse the pain and suffering it has inflicted on so many individuals and groups of people. It takes courage to accept our own culpability, whether directly or indirectly, in tainting, obscuring, and violating the image of God in those whom we have otherized. It also takes courage to confront resistance from those who hold tightly and rigidly to their religious beliefs and to persevere in the face of those who look the other way or "pass on the other side." As well, it takes a generous spirit and openheartedness to welcome those who are different from us, to see them as guests bearing gifts that will widen our horizon of understanding of what it means to be a member of the human family in all its complexity and diversity. This attitude of hospitality places a premium on the divine nature that is present in all of us, which places us all on equal footing before the divine and bestows upon us divine compassion and love in equal measure. It is in this spirit that we can enter into genuine dialogue and offer each other utmost respect and esteem even in our differences and disagreements. Lastly, it takes discipline to harness our capacity for compassionate response. The change we wish to make requires hard work and dedication, and this means training our mind and heart without ceasing until we reach a stage where compassion becomes a way of life for us. In so doing, we also make an impression on our brain, which will mediate and support our efforts towards this end. The task is daunting but never impossible or to be carried out alone. We need the support and encouragement of our faith community to spur us on, to partner with us in this radical expression of incarnating God amidst a broken and suffering world.

The compassion meditation practice in this section is divided into three parts. The first one is a meditation that allows for an opportunity to reflect on or be mindful of ways that we have participated in otherization and to begin the process of healing and repair. The second exercise focuses on extending compassion towards those who inflicted pain and suffering on us because we, too, have been labeled as an "other." The last exercise is meant to extend compassion towards all those who have been otherized because of their gender, race, sexual orientation, and the like, and to reflect on concrete ways to alleviate their suffering.

Compassion for a Challenging Other: Forgiveness & Repair

- Sit in a comfortable chair in a quiet space, eyes either slightly open or gently closed.

- Place your hands on your lap with your palms facing up.

- Take a few deep breaths.

- Become mindful or aware of the air that is coming into and going out of your body, of your chest rising during the in-breath and collapsing on the out-breath. Linger here for a moment.

- Whenever you find yourself getting lost in your head or distracted, no problem, no judgment, and no shame. Gently draw your attention back to the sensation of breathing.

- Bring to mind a time or a situation when you have judged, looked down upon, criticized, spoken negatively, or behaved wrongly towards someone whom you consider an "other." As best as you can, imagine vividly his/her face, the tone of his/her voice, gestures, mannerisms, and demeanor.

- Look deeply into his/her eyes and begin to notice the suffering this person might be experiencing simply because of who he/she is (e.g., a woman, a Muslim, gay or lesbian, aboriginal, etc.). Become mindful of how you participate in their otherization, either directly or indirectly, and notice how this behavior is impacting the life of this person. If you were in this person's shoes, how might your own judgment make you feel? Linger here for a moment and stay with whatever feelings might arise so that you can catch a glimpse of what is like to be them—otherized, excluded, judged, and violated.

- Ask the Spirit of God to show you aspects of your life that contribute to the suffering of others and let this conviction and heightened awareness guide you towards forgiveness and repair. While breathing mindfully, utter these words to yourself:

    May I be convicted of my sin of judgment and acts of exclusion.
    May I see in every person the image of God and their sacred worth.
    May I relate to them with utmost respect that is due them.

- Repeat this prayer two more times and let these words take root in your heart and mind.

- As you end this time of meditation, think of a very tangible way of repairing this relationship that has been broken by otherization and ways that you can begin to challenge it.

- In the last few minutes, take a few deep breaths and turn your attention again to the sensation of your breathing. When ready you can open your eyes if they have been closed and direct a loving, compassionate gaze outward and into the rest of your day.

The second meditation takes its inspiration from the words and example of Jesus Christ in Luke 6:27–31:

> But to you who are listening I say: Love your enemies, do good to those who hate you, bless those who curse you, pray for those who mistreat you. If someone slaps you on one cheek, turn to them the other also. If someone takes your coat, do not withhold your shirt from them. Give to everyone who asks of you, and if anyone takes what belongs to you, do not demand it back. Do to others as you would have them do to you.

Christ's admonition to repay evil with good, to counter hate with love, and to reverse curses with blessings subverts humans' propensity to retaliate when wronged, harmed, and violated. This not only breaks the cycle of violence but it also "disarms the enemy"[9] and provides us with an opportunity to see past their injurious behavior and into the core of their humanity, which is as fragile and broken as ours. Of course, this does not excuse or explain away the pain and suffering they have caused. It merely suggests that "a life that consistently refuses to succumb to the temptation of hatred

---

9. Armstrong, *Twelve Steps to a Compassionate Life*, 181.

has an enduring power of its own."[10] A life of compassion has that enduring capacity to defeat the evil in this world not by weapons of destruction but by the power of love and human connection, one to another. With this radical approach to relating to our enemy we soften the threat systems in each other's brains and rouse our compassionate neural systems that will spark a life guided by the Golden Rule.

Compassion for a Challenging Other: Turning the Other Cheek

- Sit in a comfortable chair in a quiet space, eyes either slightly open or gently closed.
- Place your hands on your lap with your palms facing up.
- Take a few deep breaths.
- Become mindful or aware of the air that is coming into and going out of your body, of your chest rising during the in-breath and collapsing on the out-breath. Linger here for a moment.
- Whenever you find yourself getting lost in your head or distracted, no problem, no judgment, and no shame. Gently draw your attention back to the sensation of breathing.
- Bring to mind a time or a situation that you felt judged, looked down upon, criticized, spoken negatively about, or harmed because you are different, an outsider, belonging to the "out-group." Let feelings surface and be present to them. As best as you can try not to judge yourself nor be swayed or managed by their strength. Breathe through these feelings and acknowledge them for what they are—your emotional responses to the pain and suffering to which you have been subjected. You may feel anger towards those who manifested these feelings, and for good reason. That is perfectly appropriate and understandable. Be mindful of these feelings and breathe through them as you become conscious of them.
- Now get in touch with your compassionate self—the part of you that is secure and rooted in God's love for you, that reminds you of your belovedness despite how other people may treat or relate to you. Identify with and lean into the innate qualities of your compassionate

10. Ibid., 183.

self—empathic, accepting, awake, benevolent, especially in the face of suffering, and mindful at all times. Linger here for a moment until you experience the warm embrace of your compassionate self.

- Imagine the face of the person who did you wrong. Look deeply into his/her eyes and become aware of this person's story and history. Reflect on how much his/her social context, cultural upbringing, religious affiliation, and his/her own vulnerabilities, insecurities, fears, ignorance, and own suffering has shaped and contributed to his prejudicial and damaging behaviors. As you reflect on these things pay attention to whatever feelings may surface within you and attend to them with curiosity and hospitality. Let your compassionate self be the vessel of these feelings and let this part of you offer the strength and inspiration that you need to offer these words to this person.

  [Say the person's name], may you be free from the destructive effects of hatred and hostility.

  May you see and appreciate the sacred worth and image of God in each person.

  May you radiate love, acceptance, and kindness to all.

- Repeat this prayer two more times and let these words take root in your heart and mind.

- As you end this time of meditation, think of a very tangible way of extending grace, forgiveness, and compassion towards this person.

- In the last few minutes, take a few deep breaths and turn your attention again to the sensation of your breathing. When ready you can open your eyes if they have been closed and direct a loving, compassionate gaze outward and into the rest of your day.

Lately, we have been shaken by incidences around the world of individuals and people groups who have been killed mercilessly or suffered tremendously at the hands of extremists of various persuasions—from political to religious to personal. People have been profiled and targeted because of their race, religion, gender, and sexual orientation and they, along with their families and loved ones, suffered excruciating pain and agony. We offer this meditation as a way of raising our consciousness towards the suffering of our brothers and sisters who are all part of our human family.

Compassion for our Human Family

- Sit in a comfortable chair in a quiet space, eyes either slightly open or gently closed.

- Place your hands on your lap with your palms facing up.

- Take a few deep breaths.

- Become mindful or aware of the air that is coming into and going out of your body, of your chest rising during the in-breath and collapsing on the out-breath. Linger here for a moment.

- Whenever you find yourself getting lost in your head or distracted, no problem, no judgment, and no shame. Gently draw your attention back to the sensation of breathing.

- Become aware of individuals—young or old, man or woman, Christian, Jew, or Muslim, straight, gay, lesbian or transgendered, Aboriginal, black, Hispanic, white, or Asian, whatever the case may be—who have been subjected to torture, killing, discrimination, assault, and other forms of cruelty and violence by others. Notice whatever feelings this may evoke within you and simply acknowledge their existence. If and when you feel empathy and compassion attend to these feelings and allow them to expand within you.

- As you lean into the feeling of compassion towards the suffering of our human family, offer these words.

  May you all experience relief and healing from your suffering.
  May you find the strength within you to withstand your pain.
  May you experience the comforting and compassionate presence of
  God during this time of tumult, persecution, and affliction.

- Repeat this prayer two more times and let these words take root in your heart and mind.

- As you end this time of meditation, think of a very tangible way of extending compassion to someone who is suffering in this manner whether near or far.

- In the last few minutes, take a few deep breaths and turn your attention again to the sensation of your breathing. When ready you can open your eyes if they have been closed and direct a loving, compassionate gaze outward and into the rest of your day.

. . . .

EXERCISE SEVEN: COMPASSION FOR ALL SENTIENT BEINGS

Setting the Context

The creation narrative in the first two chapters of Genesis reminds us of our utter dependence on God, who brings forth and sustains our very existence along with the rest of the created order. This existence is hallowed by virtue of our standing before God, that is, we are all created in the image of God and are called to represent, mediate, and incarnate the character of God on earth. This call to faithful stewardship entails a particular presence for particular moments in our life together. The third chapter of Genesis paints a rather bleak picture of the state of humanity and God's creation after the fall. Estrangement ensues and suffering of all kinds follows with devastating results. Yet, in the midst of all this the image of God that is etched deeply in every human being remains, though perhaps obscured or tainted. The shadow of sin that blanketed all of creation is juxtaposed with a flicker of light that is in all of us and then completely driven away by the light of the world.

We keep this light aflame as our way of responding to God's call to be light to the world (Matt 5:14), the world that so often swells with much pain and suffering. And so we let this light of compassion shine before all of creation and all sentient beings without reservations or conditions. Yes, this call to compassion is boundless and inexhaustible, the same way that God's love for his creation is boundless and inexhaustible. When we mirror God's compassionate heart to the world others will witness our good deeds and glorify our Father in heaven (Matt 5:16).

The last meditation offered in this section reminds us of our deep connection with creation as well as our common or shared responsibility to care for one another.

> After the world wars, genocide, and terrorism of the twentieth
> century, the purpose of the tribe or the nation can no longer be to

fight, dominate, exploit, conquer, colonize, occupy, kill, convert or terrorize rival groups. We have a duty to get to know one another, and to cultivate a concern and responsibility for all our neighbors in the global village.[11]

Cultivating compassion for everyone begins in the interior of our heart and expands to our distant neighbors whom we may not meet face-to-face but whose humanity we share and regard with utmost value and respect. After all, when we imagine their human faces we encounter the very face of God.

Compassion for All Sentient Beings

- Sit in a comfortable chair in a quiet space, eyes either slightly open or gently closed.

- Place your hands on your lap with your palms facing up.

- Take a few deep breaths.

- Become mindful or aware of the air that is coming into and going out of your body, of your chest rising during the in-breath and collapsing on the out-breath. Linger here for a moment.

- Whenever you find yourself getting lost in your head or distracted, no problem, no judgment, and no shame. Gently draw your attention back to the sensation of breathing.

- Become aware of all people and all created beings both near and far. Remind yourself of our shared beginnings as one created lovingly and caringly by God and whose image is in all of us. Notice whatever feelings and thoughts may come up as you remember your deep connection with God and the rest of his creation. With a half-smile, silently utter these words:

    May all of God's creation be glad and rejoice.
    May we all live in peace and harmony.
    May we see the face of God in each other.

- Repeat this prayer two more times and let these words take root in your heart and mind.

11. Ibid., 144.

- Now imagine holding a lit candle that symbolizes Christ who is light and love and who cares deeply for the well-being of God's creation. Imagine the light shining and spreading through all of creation, driving away darkness and healing all pain and suffering. As you see the light of Christ breaking through and transforming all of creation, offer these words:

  May this light illumine and heal your pain and suffering.
  May you feel the compassionate presence of Christ in your life.
  May you have courage, grace, and peace.

- Repeat this prayer two more times and let these words take root in your heart and mind.

- As you end this time of meditation, think of a very tangible way of extending compassion to someone who is suffering whether near or far.

- In the last few minutes, take a few deep breaths and turn your attention again to the sensation of your breathing. When ready you can open your eyes if they have been closed and direct a loving, compassionate gaze outward and into the rest of your day.

A story from the desert fathers is quite fitting as we draw this little book on compassion to a close.

> There were two monks who committed a very serious sin when they went to the village to sell their wares. But they were wise enough not to let the devil trick them into discouragement and so they came back to the desert and went to the Abba to confess their sins. To ease them into their conversation, they were asked to go and live on their own for one month on bread and water, to pray and do penance. When the time was over, Abba himself came over to reunite them with the disciples. However he was very surprised because one came out grim, downcast and pale while the other was radiant, buoyant and brisk. "What did you meditate upon? Abba asked. The sad monk answered: "I thought constantly on the punishment which I merit and the justice of God." The happy monk answered: "Well, I used to remind myself constantly the mercy of God and the love which Jesus Christ had for the sinner." Both of them were joyfully accepted back in the community but Abba remarked on the wisdom of the brother who his mind fixed on the compassion of God.[12]

12. "Stories of the Desert Fathers."

And in the spirit of the parable of the Good Samaritan, let us all "go and do likewise."

Bibliography

Armstrong, Karen. *Twelve Steps to a Compassionate Life*. New York: Random House, 2011.

Ashar, Yoni K. "Towards a neuroscience of compassion: a brain systems-based model and research agenda." *wagerlab.colorado.edu*.

Avananti, Alessio, et al. "Racial bias reduce empathic sensorimotor with other race-pain." *Current Biology* 20 (2010) 1018–20.

Baker, Augustine. "Sancta Sophia, 1657." In *Early Modern Catholicism: An Anthology of Primary Sources*, edited by Robert S. Miola, 326. Oxford: Oxford University Press, 2007.

Barrett, Justin L. *Cognitive Science Religion and Theology: From Human Minds to Divine Minds*. Conschohocken, PA: Templeton, 2011.

Batson, Daniel. *Altruism in Humans*. Oxford: Oxford University Press, 2011.

Begley, Sharon. "Scans of monks' brains show meditation alters structure and functioning." *Science Journal* (2004) B1.

Beker, J. Christian. *Suffering and Hope*. Philadelphia: Fortress, 1987.

Big Hero 6. Dir. Don Hall and Chris Williams. Disney, 2014. Film.

Bowlby, John. *Attachment and Loss*. 2nd ed. New York: Basic, 1983.

Brown, Warren S., and Brad D. Strawn. *The Physical Nature of the Christian Life: Neuroscience, Psychology and the Church*. Cambridge: Cambridge University Press, 2012.

Byrne, Brendan. *The Hospitality of God: A Reading of Luke's Gospel*. Collegeville, MN: Liturgical, 2000.

Carson, Donald A. *How Long, O Lord: Reflections on Suffering and Evil*. 2nd ed. Nottingham: InterVarsity, 2006.

Carter, Rita. *The Human Brain Book*. New York: DK Penguin/Random House, 2009.

Clarke, Peter. *All in the Mind? Does Neuroscience Challenge Faith?* Oxford: Lion, 2015.

Cikara, Mina, et al. "Us and Them: Intergroup failures of empathy." *Current Directions in Psychological Science* 20:3 (2011) 149–53.

Cure for Love. Dir. Francine Pelletier & Christina Willings. NFB, 2008. Film.

Danker, Frederick William., ed. *A Greek Lexicon of the NT and other Early Christian Literature*. 3rd ed. Chicago: University of Chicago Press, 2000.

Davidson, Richard, et al. "Neuroplasticity and Meditation." *IEEE Signal Magazine* 25 (2008) 176.

Delio, Ilia. *Compassion: Living in the Spirit of St. Francis*. Cincinnati: St. Anthony Messenger, 2011.

Dornisch, Loretta. *A Woman Reads the Gospel of Luke*. Collegeville, MN: Liturgical, 1996.

Duerden, Emma, et al. "Lateralization of affective processing in the insula." *NeuroImage* 78 (2013) 159–75.

Dunbar, Robin. "The social brain: Mind, language, and society in evolutionary perspective." *Annual Review of Anthropology* 43 (2009) 163–81.

Ellis, Marie. "Mapping emotions in the body yields consistent global results." *Medicalnewstoday.com*, January 4, 2014.

Elwell, Walter A., ed. *Evangelical Dictionary of Biblical Theology*. Grand Rapids: Baker, 1996.

Fabricatore, Daniel J. *Form of God, Form of Servant: An Examination of the Greek Noun μορφη in Philippians 2:6–7*. Lanham, MD: University Press of America, 2010.

Flemming, Dean. *Philippians: A Commentary in the Wesleyan Tradition*. Kansas City, MO: Beacon Hill, 2009.

Fosha, Diana, Daniel J. Segel, and Mariod F. Solomon, eds. *The Healing Power of Emotion: Affective Neuroscience, Development & Clinical Practice*. New York: W.W. Norton, 2009.

Frith, Chris, et al. "The neural basis of mentalizing." *Neuron* 50 (2006) 531–34.

For the Bible Tells Me So. Dir. Daniel G. Karslake. First Run Features, 2007. Film.

Gilbert, Paul, and Choden. *Mindful Compassion*. Oakland, CA: New Harbinger, 2014.

Goetz, Jennifer, et al. "Compassion: An Evolutionary Analysis and Empirical Review." *Psychological Bulletin* 136:3 (2010) 354.

Goldberg, Carl. *On Being a Psychotherapist*. Northvale, NJ: Jason Aronson, 1997.

"Great Philosophers: Augustine on Evil." *Oregonstate.edu*, InterQuest.

Greathouse, William M. *Romans 9–16: A Commentary in the Wesleyan Tradition*. Kansas City, MO: Beacon Hill, 2008.

Green, Joshua, et al. "An fMRI investigation of emotional engagement in moral judgment." *Science* 293 (2001) 2105–8.

Gregory, R. L., ed. *The Oxford Companion to the Mind*. Oxford: Oxford University Press, 1987.

Haber, Suzanne, et al. "The reward circuit: linking primate autonomy and human imaging." *Neuropsychopharmacology* 35 (2010) 4–26.

Happold, Frederick C. *Mysticism: A Study and an Anthology*. London: Penguin, 1973.

Harmon-Jones, Eddie, and Jennifer Beer, eds. *Methods in Social Neuroscience*. New York: Guilford, 2009.

Hebblethwaite, Brian. *Evil, Suffering and Religion*. London: Sheldon, 1976.

Hultgren, Arland J. *Paul's Letter to the Romans: A Commentary*. Grand Rapids: Eerdmans, 2011.

Immordino-Yang, Mary Helen, et al. "Neural correlates of admiration and compassion." *Proceedings of the National Academy of Sciences USA* 106 (2009) 8021–26.

Jeeves, Malcolm. *Minds, Brains, Souls and Gods: A Conversation on Faith, Psychology and Neuroscience*. Downers Grove, IL: InterVarsity, 2013.

Jeeves, Malcolm, and Warren S. Brown. *Neuroscience Psychology and Religion: Illussion, Delusions, and Realities about Human Nature*. Conschohocken, PA: Templeton, 2009.

Juergensmeyer, Mark. *Terror in the Mind of God: The Global Rise of Religious Violence*. Los Angeles: University of California Press, 2001.

John of the Cross. *The Ascent of Mount Carmel and the Dark Night*. Translated by John Venard. Darlington, UK: Darlington Carmel, 1981.

Just, Arthur A. *Luke 9:51–24:53: Concordia Commentary: A Theological Exposition of Sacred Scripture*. Saint Louis: Concordia, 1997.

Kabat-Zinn, Jon. *Full Catastrophe Living: Using the Wisdom of Your Body and Mind to Face Stress, Pain and Illness*. New York: Dell, 1990.

Kazen, Thomas. *Emotions in Biblical Law: A Cognitive Science Approach*. Sheffield: Sheffield Phoenix, 2011.

Keltner, Dacher. "The Compassionate Instinct." *Greatergood.berkeley.edu*. March 2004.

Keltner, Dacher, and James Gross. "Functional accounts of emotion." *Cognition and Emotion* 13 (1999) 467–80.

Krienen, Fenna, et al. "Clan mentality: evidence that the medial prefrontal cortex responds to close others." *Journal of Neuroscience* 30 (2010) 13906–15.

Lazarus, Richard. *Emotion and Adaptation*. Oxford: Oxford University Press, 1991.

Maguire, Eleanor, et al. "Navigation-related structural change in the hippocampi of taxi drivers." *Proceedings of the National Academy of Sciences* 97 (2000) 4398–403.

Marshall, Howard. *Last Supper and Lord's Supper*. Grand Rapids: Eerdmans, 1980.

Martin, Ralph. *A Hymn of Christ: Philippians 2:5–11 in Recent Interpretation and in the Setting of Early Christian Worship*. Downers Grove, IL: InterVarsity, 1997.

McGilchrist, Ian. *The Master and His Emissary: The Divided Brain and the Making of the Western World*. New Haven, CT: Yale University Press, 2012.

McNamara, Patrick. *The Neuroscience of Religious Experience*. New York: Cambridge University Press, 2014.

Motyer, J. Alec. *The Message of Philippians*. Downers Grove, IL: InterVarsity, 1984.

Nadella, Raj. *Dialogue Not Dogma: Many Voices in the Gospel of Luke*. New York: T & T Clark, 2011.

Neff, Kristen. *Self-Compassion: Stop Beating Yourself Up and Leave Insecurity Behind*. New York: HarperCollins, 2011.

Nolasco, Rolf. *The Contemplative Counselor: A Way of Being*. Minneapolis: Fortress, 2011.

Noll, Mark A. *Jesus Christ and the Life of the Mind*. Grand Rapids: Eerdmans, 2011.

Nouwen, Henry J. M., et al. *Compassion: A Reflection on the Christian Life*. New York: Doubleday, 2005.

The Overnighters. Dir. Jesse Moss. Drafthouse, 2014. Film.

Pace, Thaddeus W. W., et al. "Effect of compassion meditation on neuroendocrine, innate, immune and behavioral responses to psychosocial stress." *Psychoneuroendocrinology* 34 (2009) 87–98.

Pew Research Center, "Religious Beliefs Underpin Opposition to Homosexuality." *Pewforum.org*. Pew Research Center, November 18, 2003.

———. "Support for Same-Sex Marriage Record High, but Key Segments Remain Opposed." *Pewforum.org*. Pew Research Center, June 8, 2015.

Pfaff, Donald W. *The Altruistic Brain: How We Are Naturally Good*. Oxford: Oxford University Press, 2015.

Pierce, Brian J. *We Walk the Path Together: Learning from Thich Nhat Hanh and Meister Eckhart*. Maryknoll: Orbis, 2005.

Porges, Stephen. *The Polyvagal Theory: Neurophysiological Foundations of Emotions, Attachment, Communication, Self Regulation*. New York: W. W. Norton, 2011.

Post, Stephen. *Unlimited Love: Altruism, Compassion, and Service*. West Conschohocken, PA: Templeton, 2003.

Resseguie, James L. *Narrative Criticism of the New Testament: An Introduction*. Grand Rapids: Baker, 2009.

Ricard, Matthew. *Altruism: The Power of Compassion to Change Yourself and the World*. London: Little, Brown, 2015.

Roy, Mathieu, et al. "Ventromedial prefrontal sub-cortical systems and the generation of affective meaning." *Trends in Cognitive Science* 16 (2012) 147–56.

Schreiner, Thomas R. *Romans: Baker Exegetical Commentary on the New Testament.* Grand Rapids: Baker, 1998.

Sepalla, Emma M., et al. "Breathing-based meditation decreases posttraumatic stress disorder symptoms in U.S. Military Veterans: A randomized controlled longitudinal study." *Journal of Traumatic Stress* 27 (2014) 397–504.

———. "Loving-kindness meditation: a tool to improve healthcare provider compassion, resilience, and patient care." *Journal of Compassionate Healthcare* 1 (2014) 1–9.

———. "Social connection and compassion: Important predictors of health and well-being." *Social Research* 80 (2013) 411–30.

Siegel, Daniel. *The Developing Mind: How Relationships and the Brain Interact to Shape Who We Are.* 2nd ed. New York: Guilford, 2012.

———. *The Mindful Brain: Reflection and Attunement in the Cultivation of Well-Being.* New York: W. W. Norton, 2007.

Shamay-Tsoory, Simone G., et al. "Two systems for empathy: a double dissociation between emotional and cognitive empathy in inferior frontal gyrus versus ventromedial prefrontal lesions." *Brain: A Journal of Neurology* 132 (2009) 617–27.

Speeth, Kathless. "On Psychotherapeutic Attention." *The Journal of Transpersonal Psychology* 14 (1982) 153.

"Stories of the Desert Fathers." *Littleway.ca, FatherPius.com.*

Taylor, Kathleen. *Cruelty: Human Evil and the Human Brain.* Oxford: Oxford University Press, 2009.

Teehan, John. *In the Name of God: The Evolutionary Origins of Religious Ethics and Violence.* Oxford: Wiley-Blackwell, 2010.

Thich Nhat Hahn. *Going Home: Jesus and Buddha as Brothers.* New York: Riverhead, 1999.

Tillich, Paul. *The Courage To Be.* New Haven, CT: Yale University Press, 2000.

Villringer, Arno, et al. "Plasticity of the human brain: We never use the same brain twice." *Mpg.de.* Max Planck Institute for Human Brain and Cognitive Sciences, May 19, 2015.

Vittorio, Gallese, et. al. "Action recognition in the premotor cortex." *Brain* 119 (1996) 593–609.

World Council of Churches Faith and Order Paper No. 111: Baptism, Eucharist, and Ministry. Geneva: WCCC, 1982.

Wright, Christopher J. H. *The God I Don't Understand.* Grand Rapids: Zondervan, 2006.

Zaki, Jamil, et al. "Equitable decision making is associated with neural markers of intrinsic value." *Proceedings of the National Academy of Sciences of the United States of America* 108 (2011) 19761–66.

Index of Subjects

Made in the USA
Charleston, SC
18 November 2016